Living and Retiring in Hawaii

Living and Retiring in Hawaii

The 50th State in the 21st Century

James R. Smith, Ph.D.
Diane Smith, B.S.

iUniverse Star
New York Lincoln Shanghai

Living and Retiring in Hawaii
The 50th State in the 21st Century

iUniverse Star
an iUniverse, Inc. imprint

For information address:
iUniverse, Inc.
2021 Pine Lake Road, Suite 100
Lincoln, NE 68512
www.iuniverse.com

ISBN: 0-595-29735-8

Printed in the United States of America

Contents

Tables, Lists and Appendices

Acknowledgements

We extend our heartfelt and enduring thanks to those who provided us information, made suggestions, and volunteered information at various points in our research. Our gratitude is cheerfully extended to the following: Ken Stephensen, State President of the AARP who was helpful in providing information on AARP agenda and projects; Regional Planner and social activist Bonnie Goodell of Puna on the Big Island provided essential data and perspective, U.H. Hilo Professor of Economics Marcia Sakai for her well-timed reading lists; economist Leroy Laney for economic data and sage observations; Professor Emeritus William Carse of Hilo for initial advice and encouragement and for reading an early draft of the ms; William Takaba, Director of the Office of Aging; and attorney Ralph Black of Hilo. Special thanks go to Jessica Ernst and Phoebe Mills for assistance with the manuscript at critical points and moving it forward; and thanks to Barbara Hastings for her observations and feedback on matters stylistic and substantive. Thanks to real estate professionals Ruth Chang, Joe Correa, Phyllis Hamilton and Martin Oliver for their valuable information on Island real estate. Special appreciation to librarians Jo-Nell Palacio and Gabrielle Casart at Laupahoehoe Public Library for their research assistance and for suffering our late renewals. And to all those anonymous sources—hitchhikers and backpackers, waitresses and baggage handlers, taxi drivers and public officials, clergy and teachers, musicians and artists throughout the Islands—we extend our gratitude to each of them for being approachable, for volunteering information and for their candor and wit that became part of this book.

Twain, Stevenson, London

"The date is 1840. Scene the true Isle of the Blest: that is to say, the Sandwich Isles - to this day the peacefullest, restfullest, sunniest, balmiest, dreamiest haven of refuge for a worn and weary spirit the surface of the earth can offer. Away out there in the mid-solitudes of the vast Pacific, and far down to the edge of the tropics, they lie asleep in the waves, perpetually green and beautiful, remote from the work-day world and its frets and worries, a bloomy fragrant paradise, where the troubled may go and find peace, and the sick and tired find strength and rest. There they lie, the divine islands, forever shining in the sun, forever smiling out of the sparkling sea, with its soft mottlings of drifting cloud-shadows and vagrant cat's-paws of wind; forever inviting you, never repulsing you; and whosoever looks upon them once will never more get the picture out of his memory till he die."

Mark Twain

"I have just been a week away alone on the lee coast of Hawaii; the only white creature in many miles, riding five and a half hours one day, living with a native, seeing poor lepers shipped off to Molokai, hearing native causes and giving my opinion as amicus curiae as to the interpretation of a statute in English; a lovely week among Gods best - at least Gods sweetest - works, Polynesians. It has bettered me greatly. If I could only stay there the time that remains, I could get my work done and be happy".

Robert Louis Stevenson

"You cannot escape liking the climate...I was a young fellow, just out of college when I came here eighteen years ago...I warn you, if you have some spot dear to you on earth, not to linger here too long, else you will find this dearer".

Jack London

Prologue: How This Book Came to Be Written

Our story is not an unusual one. Thousands have preceded us, and tens of thousands will succeed us in making Hawaii a second home, a home-away-from-home, or a permanent vacation, retirement or respite site.

There is no saga, tale of woe, or trail of tears to mark our progression. Only the joy of exploring Hawaii, the romance of doing so together, and an occasional sore back or smashed thumb from refurbishing and landscaping our choice of housing and habitat.

When I left my hometown of Kansas City, Missouri, in January of 1963, it was 12 degrees above zero and a snowstorm was in progress. Twelve hours later I stepped off a Pan Am jet at Honolulu International Airport into warm, moist air of 74 degrees filled with fragrances from the dozens of leis being given to the descending passengers. Hawaii was a different place.

In 1963 there was no International Market Place, no Polynesian Cultural Center, no Sea Life Park and no Kahala Hilton. Makaha, already famous for its surf, was still a beach with dirt roads and no resorts. The Hilton Hawaiian Village looked and smelled new. The International Market Place was the entertainment site *du jour*, as a youthful Don Ho reigned supreme. Haunauma Bay was clean and clear, hosting only a few dozen sun worshippers and neophyte snorkelers. One could not only park there for free but Hanauma Bay was often the scene of all night revelry. There was no curfew.

In 1963 there were no topless bars, no satellite TV, no PC links, no convention center, no Aloha Stadium, no Magic Island and no wide body jet liners. The new East-West Center was not yet staffed; there were fewer student applicants than scholarship slots. The Ala Moana shopping center stores were just being opened. The Blaisdell Center, only recently funded, was to undergo more than two years of construction which would proceed a gala premiere in 1964. The University of Hawaii at Manoa had just over ten thousand students and no out of state tuition. One could still park a car on campus without a fee or fine! The conversion of the Lunalilo Freeway to Interstate Highway 1 was just being started. Many now familiar landmarks on Oahu and elsewhere were visions not yet planned. The populace, which was considerably less than one million residents, was still heady with the attainment of statehood.

Like Jack London, I was a young fellow, just out of college with the world seemingly before me, recently embarked on what would become a life-long love affair with the islands of Hawaii. Apparently, I stayed long enough to make Hawaii more dear than my birthplace.

As a graduate student at the University of Hawaii I had a third floor walk-up apartment within yards of the campus. The street was appropriately named Sea View Avenue and from my tiny lanai I could see Diamond Head, most of Waikiki and much of downtown Honolulu with Pearl Harbor far in the distance. Today, that lanai affords a wonderful view of…other lanais. By 1983, Sea View Avenue was a misnomer, victim to view pollution, and there was no longer a view of the sea to speak of from Sea View Avenue. Development and condominium construction had taken its toll as this scenario came to be repeated ad nauseum the length and breadth of Oahu.

James R. Smith, Ph.D. Diane Smith, B.S.

In 1991 an unforeseen set of personal and family circumstances created an opportunity to travel from our home in Berkeley, California to Hawaii with my wife Diane, a California native, to seriously consider the Islands as a retirement site. Diane had traveled to Hawaii on several occasions and had an abiding interest in living here. Hawaii called to us together as it had earlier called to me solo voce.

In 1992, after considerable exploration and deliberation, we purchased a "fixer" on the Hamakua Coast of the Big Island, which we repaired, rehabilitated and refurbished. We found our island home, a compact three bedroom A-frame with an ocean view, located in a former plantation village bounded by mountain streams and surrounded by sugar cane fields with Mauna Kea looming majestically in the background. Idyllic? Well, we think so.

To aid our transition to retirement in Hawaii, we looked for information resources with insights into Hawaii's economy, politics and culture. The extant literature did not provide what we sought; what was available was either dated or irrelevant.[i] There has been no sustained inquiry into retirement prospects in Hawaii since 1983.

While we were not, as many writers allege, compelled to write this book, we were motivated to catch up on thirty years of Hawaii, to validate our choice of the Big Island as a prospective retirement site, and to appreciate and foresee the future of the Islands as an affordable and sustainable home. These efforts began with travel notes and nocturnal journal entries which have been synthesized into this book. These journal entries, supplemented by State of Hawaii Data sources, United States Census Data, real estate surveys and population studies, interview material and articles and anecdotes culled from local publications and newspapers throughout Hawaii, constitute the substance of our efforts. We hope it is helpful to retirees as they make one of life's bittersweet choices: where and how to retire.

The material presented here aims to help you decide whether to retire in Hawaii. It is our intent to assist those interested in Hawaii as a retirement site whether you already live here or not. Throughout the book we have tried to address the question: Is Hawaii retiree friendly?

We have tried to answer the questions we had when we investigated our retirement options as well as questions from others curious about living and retiring in Hawaii. We share information found in many sources—both within the narrative and as tables or appendices. Website and E-links, as well as selected phone numbers, are included.

While the book is admittedly partial to the Big Island of Hawaii in some respects, there are no specific endorsements. Even the restaurants and locales in our "top ten" lists should be viewed as a matter of personal taste rather than advertisements. Our preference for the Orchid Isle and the Hamakua Coast was based on our desire for open space, a modest budget, and a desire for a sub-tropical environment in a rural setting. We make no pretense to thoroughness and no claim to objectivity. Our approach is admittedly that of an interested observer but one with firsthand experience and a long-term perspective. Each island would sustain volumes; a second volume devoted to the Big Island is underway.[ii]

All facts and events are put forth in good faith and to the best of our knowledge. The conclusions are our own based on such information and advice and knowledge gleaned in the course of research during 1998-2000.

We suggest the reader use this book as a springboard for information gathering, personal research, and, ultimately, decision-making about retirement in general and Hawaii in particular. We hope it not only informs your retirement decision, but that in seeking an answer you find, as we did, whatever it is your heart desires.

Introduction: Paradise Revisited, Paradise Revised: A Philosopher's Perspective

The search for an earthly Paradise is commonplace among writers, adventurers, and explorers throughout history and around the world. What is it they seek? What are the common elements of their desires? What is their motivation?

Mark Twain, Robert Louis Stevenson and Jack London each wrote eloquent prose in praise of the Pacific paradise we know as Hawaii. These literary figures experienced the islands of Hawaii with what can be seen in hindsight as a common purpose—the search for peace combined with plenty, for natural and human beauty, for adventure, serenity, peace of mind and, not least, a congenial and stimulating place to write. They fed the imagination of countless readers, stoking the mythology of Hawaii and the romantic legend that life in Hawaii is somehow better, more wholesome, more exciting, more fulfilling, than other places—even warm and sunny places—elsewhere.

What were Stevenson, Twain and London seeking? Nothing less than what we and you and thousands of other less prominent explorers and travelers, including would-be retirees, seek. Some personal vision of Paradise? Perhaps. The good life according to our lights, sights, and expectations? Perhaps. Today's pundits might say that we are all seeking a "healing environment," an "integrated lifestyle" or a "self-actualized way of life." In the end, it's a matter of perspective and hair-splitting. We seek love, leisure, security, good health and abundance, not always in that order.

The collective perception of Twain, Stevenson and London became the western world's view of Hawaii—primitive, lush, beautiful beyond words, enchanting beyond belief, welcoming beyond imagination. While this image lingers, the Hawaii of these literary figures has been transformed and in many respects is nearly gone. In spite of an overflow of tourists and in spite of "economic development" bordering on environmental piracy and in spite of the dual processes of gentrification and ghettoization reinforcing social stratification, Hawaii still affords some justification for the reputation as a Paradise on Earth. Paradise, let us observe at the outset, is a state of mind, not a place; it is a matter properly for psychology and mythology rather than geography or even theology.

The Paradise theme is ubiquitous in Hawaiian legend and lore, and even more pronounced or exploited in the 21st century sub-culture of tourism. In Hawaii we encounter not only Paradise Plants and Paradise Tours and Paradise Wedding, but with equal aplomb Paradise Plumbing, Paradise Taxi and Paradise Massage. Clearly, nothing much is sacred in this contemporary earth-bound paradise.

It is of particular note that one of the several definitions of paradise given in the Oxford English Dictionary is of paradise as a "pleasure garden."[iii] What better characterizes Hawaii than that? Hawaii, with its beaches and mountains, its valleys and rain forests, is as close to a paradise garden—and as close to an adult theme park, or a playground of nature, a ludenic[iv] park, —as man and nature will allow. It is with irony that Kauai is locally known as the Garden Island. Truth to tell, all the islands are lush, rugged, pastoral and sub-tropical in climate and environment.

James R. Smith, Ph.D. Diane Smith, B.S.

A worthwhile approach to discussions of retirement, phased, partial or terminal, in Hawaii is by way of the theory of <u>ludenics</u>.[v] Hawaii celebrates and promotes the idea of adult play. The climate, geography and culture, ancient and modern, invite us to immerse ourselves in nature, to engage in playful pursuits from surfing and swimming, to golf and tennis, and all manner of adventure, sport, and recreation. From this point of view Hawaii is, in brief, a <u>ludenic</u>[vi] culture, one founded on the relative absence of toil and the presence of play behaviors and play-oriented institutions. In "ancient" Hawaii, i.e. pre-contact (1778) what did the chiefs (ali'i) and royalty of Hawaii do? As elsewhere, when the combination of security and abundance were met, the leisure class, those of royalty and noble rank played and played—sport, games, food festivals: an entire culture devoted to pleasurable pursuits. No wonder, then, that millions come to Hawaii to seek leisure, recreation, and retirement—all opportunities to play.

Retirement is often conceived as a time to play—to recreate, to seek one's second childhood, to explore and travel as an adult, with whatever adult trappings and equipage one can lawfully muster in a lifetime of work.

There is industry in Hawaii to be sure. But it is geared and driven by tourism, and oriented toward play and leisure pursuits. In that limited and qualified sense, Hawaii is a contemporary and revised version of Paradise.

So, we have a Paradise before us, a pleasure garden for all ages really, but available to retirees at a special time of life and in a special way. It is a Paradise that is evolving, suffering irreversible change and possible terminal development. When we revisit the Paradise that is Hawaii we today revisit a Paradise vastly revised. What we encounter in contemporary Hawaii is a secular, perhaps even profane Paradise, a Paradise still in transition, a Paradise after the fall, as it were.[vii]

Hawaii has been undergoing a multifaceted and multiphased process of change for over 200 years (beginning with western contact in 1778). The former island kingdom and feudal economy of Hawaii now participates directly, reciprocally, and as a full constitutional partner with the mightiest and wealthiest nation in the world. It is a kingdom turned colony turned territory turned sovereign State with all the rights, rules, and responsibilities pertaining thereto. Hawaii's history is now a chapter in American and in world history, several dots on a map that are as close to Eden as any ordinary sinner is likely to get. We can indulge these fantasies productively so long as we keep in mind that the search for paradise, if it is anything other than the mad rush of fools, is the stuff of which dreams are made.

Hawaii was once the symbol of paradise around the world, an image of incomparable beauty and an unending leisure. Hawaii hosts a culture in pursuit of arts, sports, a community bound together by *aloha*, a love of the land and strong sense of *ohana* (family ties). But we are now in the 21st century and thus led to pursue a paradise whose image is somewhat tarnished.

A revealing and persuasive illustration of Hawaii revised and abused is Haunauma Bay. Once a pristine natural attraction located on East Oahu it was enjoyed by local residents and tourists alike. Swimmers and sunbathers communed with sun and sand. Boy scouts camped there; lovers parked there, it was often the site of nocturnal activities neither supervised nor effectively patrolled. The local curfew was not enforced. The waves poured over nude swimmers under a blanket of stars by night and picnickers and bathers by day. It was the site of countless neophyte snorkelers encountering innumerable species in a safe and secure aquatic environment.

Now the area is closed at night, and one pays for parking (if available), shuttle service and $3.00 for bottled water. There is no drinking (yeah, sure), no feeda da fish, and the hiking perimeter (where I many times hiked for a good photo of the bay) is closed to visitors.

Malia Zimmerman[viii] mourns for the picnics and snorkeling of her childhood. But upon taking her six year old boy to the bay she encountered "…coral, once vibrant, was [now] a slimy brown. The fish, once swarming and colorful, were scarce and grayed. And the eels and sea urchins were almost non-existent. 'where's the fish?' my son kept asking."

Haunauma bay is now polluted with depleted fish schools, and a ruination disguised as "natural" by carefully placed rocks and designer foot paths from which one dare not stray. It resembles a movie set with a touch of Disneyland. We regard the bay as a national treasure turned into an environmental tragedy, one among many in paradise revised.

What does this have to do with your retirement? Plenty. This paradise, revised in all its aspects, will determine the quality of life of those who choose to live here. Our own vision and version of paradise is what most of us, consciously or unconsciously, seek as we retire. And if not paradise, then some form of happiness, bliss, and/or fulfillment, transient or enduring, that allows us to age, if not gracefully, at least with a minimum of pain and suffering.

Hawaii is a prime locale for such a life as those who reside here know and widely agree. Those yet to come—and there will be many—will change the face of Hawaii perhaps as never before. We believe Hawaii will become a major retirement site during the first half of the 21st century and that this will again transform life and living in the Islands.

Chapter 1

Basic Considerations: Why Hawaii? Is Hawaii Retiree Friendly?

Retiring in Hawaii can be an adventure, a wonderful daily tonic, a place for exciting personal growth. The decision may be based on emotion, but we recommend you support it with sound information, common sense and, above all, reflection upon whatever it is that moves you and yours.

We chose Hawaii for several important reasons. Foremost, of course, is the climate. With an annual temperature averaging 70 - 85 degrees throughout the islands, it is entirely possible to enjoy the outdoors year-round. In *Retirement Edens* Peter A. Dickinson remarks, "the climate has a lot to do with it…the older we get, the more difficulty we have in adjusting to drastic changes in climate."[ix] Another selling point is the natural beauty with which the islands are blessed. Majestic mountains intertwine with white and black-sand beaches, striking waterfalls, molten volcanoes, and lush plant life, making way for a truly earthly sub-tropical Paradise. Finally, we came because of the culture here. Life in the islands is less frenetic, slower, and the people of the islands tend to be elder-friendly.

In *Retirement Living*, Sally Ravel and Lee Ann Wolfe write "considering that this may be a lifetime decision, it is essential that you make a judgment that will provide an optimum living situation for you."[x]

Knowing we wanted to live here was only the beginning of the story. Our decision could not have been made without heavily weighing our options and deciding which island, coast and community was right for us. After researching prospective areas at length on repeat visits, we decided the island of Hawaii (also known as the Big Island and The Orchid Isle) was our <u>optimum</u> choice.

While we are definitely comfortable living in Hawaii, only you can decide if you'll find happiness here. In *How To Retire in Hawaii on a Lot Less Than You'd Think*, psychologist Joseph Bratton addresses these considerations about living in Hawaii: [xi]

1. Affordability—Do we/I have enough money?
2. Climate—Can we find a climate zone that feels comfortable? Is our health compatible with that climate?
3. Dependence on Mainland Family and Friends—Can we live happily without family contacts? Or can we afford a huge phone bill?
4. Physical and Mental Stimulation—Is recreation and entertainment sufficient to maintain mental and physical health?
5. Budgeting for Neighbor Island Travel—Island Fever is not just a myth. People do suffer from homesickness, or lack of seasonal variations. (They miss the snow or changing leaves.) Some find the pace of life agonizingly slow.
6. Research—The more information you digest, the more likely you are to make a decision befitting your personal earnings, capabilities and particular lifestyle.

To these we add the questions of aging. Will you still be able to drive? Will you still be able to see? Will you need "assisted living?" Will you be living with someone or might you be living alone or caring for a loved one?

One factor that outweighs most others is cost. Most people assume that living in Hawaii is universally and outrageously expensive. They note inflated real estate prices and state-imposed excise, room and income taxes. They complain about the time, cost and distance involved in traveling to the middle of the Pacific Ocean. They also cite the high cost of goods such as gasoline, prime rib dinners and imported wine. Many believe the leisure and recreation Hawaii offers is available solely to those who can afford it.

However, those who would characterize the people of Hawaii as money-laden, indulgent and even opulent fail to perceive the realities of ordinary life. Their view is as one sees it from a tour bus: one snapshot and one pit stop at a time. They don't see people going to work, class or church, rather they focus on *luau*, beach activities, and golf. Despite a tourist brochure that boasts: "Life in Hawaii is an endless *luau*," it is not.

While the cost of living in Hawaii *is* higher than the Mainland, it is comparable to many expensive U.S. cities such as San Francisco, New York, Washington D.C. or Miami. If you plan to relocate to Hawaii with less than a thirty thousand dollar per year income, it will require major adjustments in your consumer habits and spending priorities. Be prepared to spend and consume less, cut corners, cut coupons or cut bait. Despite the higher cost of living, there are thousands of people in Hawaii doing moderately well on fixed and limited incomes.

Don't be deterred by the distance either. There are daily flights to the mainland—and all parts of the world, for that matter. In fact, Hawaii is actually closer to the California coast than California is to New York or Florida. It is easier, faster and cheaper to fly from Los Angeles to Honolulu than it is to fly from Los Angeles to the East Coast. Aloha Airlines has recently added direct flights to and from Oakland, California and Las Vegas.

Depending on the island you choose, you will find wide variations in housing and land prices, and even greater variations in accessibility to social and medical services. Select services may not be available on some islands. Health care facilities are spread thin on the rural islands, and some residents must travel to Honolulu for dental care or surgery. Those seeking night life and action will find it in what locals refer to as "the city," Honolulu. City dwellers seeking a respite from the hectic pace of urban life will find solace on the "outer" or rural islands of Kauai, Maui, Molokai and Hawaii.

Although smog in Honolulu is rare as compared with other metropolitan areas, "vog" (volcanic fog) often plagues Kona and some other areas on the Big Island. It may preclude the Kona Coast for those with respiratory problems as an otherwise suitable retirement site.

In most cases, an assessment of each island will yield a clear favorite. You may favor a condominium in the heart of Waikiki, or upon deliberation, choose a more secluded site like west Molokai or be drawn to the agricultural areas of the "Big Island" of Hawaii. One couple we know chose a country home on the north shore of the Big Island for its spectacular ocean view; it's also an ideal place to breed and exercise their show dogs. On the other hand, we also know of a semi-retired bass player who is a stockbroker by day (which begins at three a.m. in Hawaii) and boogies three nights a week in a Honolulu disco. He resides happily in a one-bedroom condo apartment three blocks off Waikiki Beach.

Pete Weaver, author of *How to Stretch your Retirement Dollar*, offers the following advice: "if you want to move, it takes research to find the best place…rent a house and rent out your house back home. If you decide you don't like your new community, you'll always have a place to retreat to. . .(also) visit during different seasons, subscribe to local newspapers and get to know the natives."[xii]

We strongly agree with Weaver. Do not retire to Hawaii without traveling, extensively and repeatedly if possible, throughout the islands.

Be sure to weigh all factors carefully, take a good long look and read more than the travel brochures. Each neighborhood and island differ in what they have to offer. We recommend you create a rating system (one to ten) based on your individual priorities and lifestyle preferences. For example, rate health care services, recreation, taxes, services for seniors, crime and transportation. You can make a list of important financial and physical considerations and rate them accordingly as another step in the decision-making process.

Additionally, we recommend that would-be retirees review the current economic and market conditions for housing, food and entertainment, including prices prevailing in one to five years prior to relocating. The more information you have, the better equipped you will be to make a wise decision for yourself, your partner and your family. See recommended readings and websites.

Before deciding on a retirement location, it's important to ask critical questions. As we were contemplating Hawaii as a possible retirement spot, various questions arose relating to our future on these islands. The following are just a few this book will address:

1. How much will it cost?
2. Should you rent, lease or build?
3. Which island will provide the ideal environment?
4. Where are the best restaurants and entertainment?
5. What about health and hospice care?
6. What about local and state, especially property, taxes?

The cost question is one of the most frequently asked by would-be retirees. Cost is a very significant issue; we recommend dealing with it first. There is no disputing the fact that Hawaii is an expensive place to live. Yet the idea that Hawaii is completely unaffordable is usually a tourist's perception. Tourists, obviously, spend more money. These same visitors assume that everyone in Hawaii spends three to four hundred dollars per day, stays in rented oceanfront properties, drives rented automobiles and seeks out the most expensive cuisine and entertainment in the islands. Not everyone in Hawaii spends like a tourist because not everyone in Hawaii is a tourist.

Cost-of-living figures are twenty to forty percent higher than most other states. Over a generation ago in *The Legend That Sells*, Bryan Farrell wrote that, among other things, the cost of imports contributes to "a cost of living roughly twenty-five percent higher than the mainland." Farrell notes that housing is also a component of higher costs. Housing in Hawaii, he says, is "a quarter to a third higher" (than the Mainland.)[xiii] Do not let these figures scare you. Your expenses will vary widely depending on your choice of island and lifestyle. Depending on your expected comfort level and financial situation, Hawaii is large and diverse enough for all types of retirement scenarios.

The good news is that Hawaii is "affordable" for at least one out of three retired couples. We contend the minimum requirement is a combined thirty thousand dollar annual income and one hundred twenty-five thousand to one hundred sixty thousand dollars "buy-in" money for a home or condominium. Some potential retirees may be blessed with more resources. Those with less should consider carefully.

Here are three possible scenarios for what one typically can buy in Hawaii (all islands—condominiums are available on Oahu for under $100,000—cabins and kit homes on neighbor islands can be found in this price range also):

Low End: $75,000 to 100,000 for a lot and cabin, or a condominium; $24,000 to $30,000 annual income necessary

Medium: $125,000 to 175,000 for a bungalow with a view; $30,000 to 40,000 annual income necessary

High End: $175,000 to 500,000 for a three- bedroom, three-bath with an ocean view on three acres; $40,000 to 100,000 annual income necessary

In order to relocate to Hawaii one must be ready and willing to pay what is locally referred to as the *price of paradise*. Bank of Hawaii economist Paul Brewbaker argues that Hawaii has a "paradise tax," which is made up of two components: cost (at twenty to forty percent) and an income penalty.[xiv] You can earn a higher salary on the mainland, particularly if you have four or more years of college. (See *Price of Paradise* for more detailed treatment.)

Not all people agree that the cost-of-living differential is so high. George Mason, a Hawaiian resident for fifty-two years and publisher emeritus of Pacific Business News, argues that the cost isn't bad, "especially when one takes into account the items not consumed by those who live in the islands." He suggests that people should "stop and think about what we don't spend our money on (snow tires, seasonal wardrobes, storm windows). The price we have to pay to live in Hawaii is decidedly offset by the myriad of plusses."[xv]

One may relocate to Hawaii for less than ten thousand dollars in moving expenses, including shipping and temporary housing. Our recommendation is that income should be about thirty thousand dollars in order to afford health insurance and medical care, basic living expenses, and a few luxuries or travel in the islands. (See Table 1-1 for a sample budget.) Others set this number somewhat lower albeit to the peril of the reader. See, e.g., *How to Live in Hawaii on $1,000 per month*, (Rico Press, Kona), a 1994 recession era bare bones approach to life in the islands. The author observes, "**you need monthly retirement or other independent income to survive on the outer islands.**"[xvi] One can do it on even less, of course, provided you omit rent and live in a tent or eliminate health insurance and live on rice and coconuts – not an enticing scenario for most senior citizens. The "hippie lifestyle," nurtured in California and elsewhere some thirty years ago, is alive and well in 21st century Hawaii suggesting that one can indeed "dropout" on less than one thousand dollars per month and still survive. We recommend it only to the young and hardy, and then only for weeks or at most for a "survivor summer." Beaches and parks are no longer available to the public for such adventures although locals are savvy to the more remote areas where prolonged camping, though not permitted, is nonetheless practiced.

In many instances, retirees will have equity in a home worth one hundred thousand dollars or more to sell there and buy here. They can also draw upon savings accounts, stock portfolios, and retirement funds or plan around such assets. They must be able to travel and be of adequate health to suffer relocation, unless they are choosing Hawaii as a rehabilitation or hospice site. Special circumstances like these will entail special expenses. However, those in sound health can relocate easily by contracting the move, seeking temporary housing prior to visiting each of the islands and making a final selection as to locale, physical environment and cost.

One of the costs included with housing is electricity, which tends to cost more for a variety of reasons—1) cost of oil and oil transportation to Hawaii 2) limited economies of scales, i.e. numbers are in the tens of thousands not hundreds of thousands, 3) cost of infrastructure. Air conditioning and refrigeration are the highest energy expenses. A majority of homes and apartments have only "open the window" air conditioning or ceiling fans. Heating bills, however, will be non-existent in most cases, unless you live in upper elevations. Supplemental systems, or thermal solar panels, are available in all areas, reducing the cost of heating water for bathing and cooking even further.

The average costs of items will vary from the U.S. Mainland and other countries. Overpriced items are usually artificially stimulated or controlled/regulated. For example, dry cereal runs four to six dollars, a gallon of milk costs about four dollars, and a loaf of bread is about $3.89. Even local fresh fish can run between seven and thirteen dollars a pound. Non-U.S. products like French wine and Mexican beer are often over-priced as well. Perishable items flown or shipped from the Mainland are more expensive in both Honolulu and the rural island stores. Fancy greens can be as much as ten dollars per pound and imported fruits and vegetables, mainly from California, are ten to twenty percent higher in the islands. Although not *over* priced, wood products, paper products and office supplies still remain expensive since they must be imported.

On the other hand, local fruits and vegetables are up to fifty percent cheaper, especially at the fresh fruit stands and farmers' markets scattered throughout the islands. (Take papayas, which sell for two dollars and fifty cents each on the Mainland, and four to six for a dollar at the open stall markets in Hawaii.) Costs in local bakeries compare favorably with Mainland bread prices, and "day-old" stores, common in many neighborhoods and villages, undercut supermarkets by as much as sixty percent or more.

You can get a good idea of average costs by looking at supermarket ads in the local newspapers, such as the *Honolulu Star Bulletin* and *The Honolulu Advertiser*. Both also have editions that cover the islands other than Oahu, and both are available on the Internet and all local papers carry sales and coupons.[xvii]

BUYING OR SHIPPING A CAR

Selection of cars for sale is better on the Mainland because there are more people on the Mainland and more cars. You have a better chance of getting the kind of car you want in the Mainland. If you have a car in good condition and with low mileage it might be worth shipping. In 1999, Matson, a major shipper to Hawaii, charged eight hundred and two dollars from San Francisco or Los Angeles to Honolulu, and eight hundred forty-two dollars to Hilo on the island of Hawaii. We sold gas-guzzlers in California and bought an '89 Toyota with forty thousand miles. State law requires registration, insurance and a safety check. Registration is by weight (a Toyota station wagon is under sixty dollars) and a safety check is fifteen dollars each year. Insurance runs six to twelve hundred dollars per year. Many elderly local residents have reported good insurance rates with AARP. The price of regular gas in Hawaii is subject to occasional shortages and some price gouging, but one can offset this with a smaller car—some of the sub-compacts get more than forty miles per gallon and electric vehicles are on the horizon. While transportation costs are higher, Hawaii residents tend to drive fewer miles.

New automobiles are one hundred percent imported and expensive, but used cars—especially from rental fleets—can be purchased at bargain prices. Remember though, sea spray contains a lot of salt, so watch out for rust! Odometer tampering is not unknown. Be aware.

TAXES

Taxes are another key factor in the cost of Paradise. In "Property Tax Fairness," T.M. Foley argues that "Hawaii has been accused of being a 'tax hell'…(Hawaii's) individual tax rate—ten percent maximum—is one of the highest in the nation."[xviii] However, California transplants, accustomed to eight percent-plus sales tax, find Hawaii's four percent General Excise Tax makes for bargain shopping. However, the tax is applied to EVERYTHING from food to medical services. Hawaii is one of the few states that taxes professional services (on gross revenues).

Property taxes in Hawaii are also lower than in California. In "Business Taxes," Jack Suyderhoud writes that "residential property tax burdens in Hawaii are relatively low, and the trend is downward."[xix]

On the Oahu, homeowners are given a property tax exemption on the first forty thousand dollars assessed value. Homeowners over the age of 55 receive a total exemption of $60,000, $80,000 at 60, and $100,000 at 65. At the age of 70, the exemption is a total of $120,000. A minimum tax of twenty-five dollars is the amount paid by many retired people in Hawaii.

For example: Leilani Jones, a retired teacher, bought her condominium for $80,000. She receives a $40K homeowner's exemption and is over 60 years of age. Her total property tax exemption is $80,000. She pays the minimum tax of $25.00 per year.

Property taxes differ by island. On the rural islands property taxes are relatively low compared to property value. For more information contact the real estate tax department, or talk to realtors for current information. See table 1-2 for property tax department information. Also see table 1-3 for property tax rates by island.

Also key to keeping costs down is planning ahead to ease your transition. For example, get a post office box and open a minimum bank account in Hawaii ahead of time. A full year ahead of a final move is not too early to begin the process of moving.

Establish a limit on your relocation budget.[xx] In 1997, two (very large) containers shipped from California cost two thousand dollars, including trucking to our house twenty-five miles from Hilo. Our approach was "minimalist"; we sold all furniture and cars, shipped household items and a few treasures and donated or disposed of the rest. It was a good way to pare down superfluous possessions.

Another frequently asked question is "which island is right for me?" One of the fascinating aspects of life in Hawaii is the diversity among the five developed and accessible islands and the unique characteristics of each. Don't assume the islands are homogenous in any respect save two: they're all warm and sunny, and as a group they are unique in their mean distance to any landmass. Besides being unique in their respective geography, economy and ethnic history, the Hawaiian Island chain is further from any landmass than any similar islands in the world. In that sense, they are remote beyond compare.[xxi]

Toni Polancy, author of *So You Want to Live in Hawaii*, recommends that unless you have a reason to choose a particular island—for example friends, or relatives or a job—you should visit at least two islands before finalizing your decision."[xxii] We strongly agree as each island, indeed, each village and valley has unique qualities and characteristics.

Each island offers something different. While the island of Oahu is a densely populated, political and commercial center, the other islands offer seclusion, serenity, and a virtually pastoral lifestyle. This is why Maui, Kauai, Molokai, Lanai and the Big Island of Hawaii are called the "outer" or "neighbor" islands. These terms, however, imply that all of Hawaii is centered on Oahu. Not so. Therefore we refer to these other islands as <u>rural islands</u> in contrast to the obvious and rampant urbanization of virtually all of Oahu that is not mountain or stream.[xxiii] While we call them rural islands, most have virtually all the modern amenities—cable TV, cell phones, internet services, etc.

Your decision rests on your needs. Maybe beaches interest you most, or you're concerned that the Bonsai Society has a large chapter, or you have a specialized health care need. All of these factors will be reflected in your decision.

Once an island is selected, the others become accessible for side trips, excursions and vacations, a wonderful bonus of living in Hawaii. Residents receive *kamaaina*[xxiv] rates, inter-island discounts on air travel and opportunities for house trades. As a resident you'll discover *luau*, fishing sites, and entertainment spots not listed in the guides.

Our number one attraction to Hawaii was the climate. Weather forecasts around the islands don't vary too much - warm and sunny, warm and cloudy, warm and rainy. "Warm" usually falls between seventy-five and eighty-five degrees. In most areas the temperature ranges are small. Most temperatures vary no more than fifteen degrees, e.g., 70-85 degrees. On the beaches, the average summer daytime high is in the mid-eighties while in winter it is still in the upper seventies. The temperatures drop about ten degrees at night.

RAINSTORMS

Despite the temperate climate, one can still find snow-capped mountains and dry desert on the island of Hawaii, and rain forests on all of the islands except Lanai. The Big Island of Hawaii is vast in comparison to the other islands, and features a variety of climatic conditions—some nine sub-climates in all—from high desert to rain forest.[xxv] Rainforests and windward coasts can be excessively humid to muggy and constantly damp. An important note is that it's a wet heat; oppressive to some; delightful to others.

After several visits and eventually residence on Hawaii's Hamakua coast we have never experienced a daytime temperature over ninety-six degrees nor a nighttime temperature lower than sixty-four degrees. If there is a winter in Hawaii as we know it on the Mainland we are unable to find it, save for the Christmas decorations at Wal-Mart, an increase in the flow of tourists and occasional accumulation of snow on the summit of Mauna Kea.

Rain can be an issue in Hawaii in certain areas. Hawaii has a drier season which corresponds with summer on the U.S. Mainland and a rainy season from November to March. Since Hawaii has a sub-tropical climate, it is almost always raining *somewhere* on one of the islands. In many areas most of the rain occurs at night. (Arranged, it would seem, by the Visitor's Bureau!)

Each of the Hawaiian Islands has a "leeward" side and a "windward" side. The leeward sides (west and south) are hotter and drier, while the windward sides (east and north) are cooler and wetter. There is no better place to observe these climate differences than on the Big Island of Hawaii. On the leeward side there are places which see only five or six inches of rain a year, while the windward side boasts the wettest American city, Hilo, with an average of one hundred and twenty inches of rain a year. The island of Kauai is home to the "wettest" spot in the world, Mt. Waialeale with an average annual rainfall of 485 inches. For a more specific account of temperature and rainfall, see Table 1-5.

The Hawaiian Islands are volcanically formed, and the islands have great variations in altitude and temperature. On Hawaii Island it sometimes snows at the summit of Mauna Kea, a 13,972-foot peak. Other upper elevations also have cooler nights, down to the low sixties occasionally dropping into the fifties.

While the weather is usually as close to perfect as anywhere on Earth, Hawaii is occasionally subjected to hurricanes and tropical storms. (The "official" hurricane season is from June through November). Hawaii is subject to two general "seasons" and four kinds of storm patterns. The seasons are known locally as Ka'u (or summer season) and Ho'oilo (or rainy, winter season). However, on some parts of some islands, e.g. North Kohala on the Big Island, and West Molokai, the differences are hardly noticeable.

The types of storms include 1) cold front storms, with strong winds from the north and northwest; 2) Kona storms, so called, because they originate mostly in the winter months from the leeward of Kona (southwest) side of the islands; 3) hurricanes and tropical storms, usually originating off the coast of Mexico and moving westward, mostly in the months from July to December; and 4) storms associated with upper-level low pressure centers, causing extensive rainfall, especially in the windward areas, like the north shore of Oahu and the Hamakua Coast of the Big Island.[xxvi] Hurricanes Iwa and Iniki in 1982 and 1992 respectively devastated Kauai and did substantial damage to parts of Niihau and Oahu. Kauai is only now recovering from the last hurricane in 1992.

Another problematic weather phenomenon that occasionally threatens Hawaii are tidal waves, known worldwide as *tsunamis.* Tsunamis are generated by distant storms and/or volcanic activity, which create large, fast-moving tidal swells, and cause flooding in low-lying areas. Killer tsunamis struck the Big Island in 1946 and 1960, causing numerous deaths, and extensive destruction. Both events are vivid in the memories of those who lived through them, and both are memorialized.[xxvii]

Fortunately for Hawaii, the National Oceanic and Atmospheric Administration (NOAA), the military, and commercial shipping provide on-going monitoring and advance warning systems. Local horns and sirens are installed in virtually all coastal areas, and the local media provide timely and accurate information as storms and tsunamis approach.

Such weather extremes, though relatively rare, are taken very seriously by local residents. Current weather conditions, including warnings and marine conditions, are continuously broadcast on AM and FM radio and cable TV, and weather is always a feature of local newscasts.

EARTHQUAKES

Between 1823 and 1959 at least 19,464 earthquakes and tremors were reported in Hawaii, with the majority occurring from 1902 to 1959. Most of them were on the Big Island, with some 800 registering a magnitude of 4.0 or more on the Richter scale. A 4.0 magnitude earthquake can cause damage and be widely felt.

Strong earthquakes have caused damage in the recent past on all islands except Kauai. Major earthquakes are the result of faulting. Since 1925 ten earthquakes with magnitudes greater than 5.3 have occurred, six on the Big Island and four on faults on the ocean floor.

Construction techniques should reflect this hazard, especially on the Island of Hawaii.

In ten years of full and part time residence we have experienced several tremors. Other than minor damage from this hazard, i.e., a few broken plates, there are no reports of major incidents.

For more information on volcanoes and earthquake, check out the following: www.co.honolulu.hi.us/, www.hawaii.gov/, http://lunahawaii:soest.hawaii.edu/cgi-bin/hawaiianwx.cgi, http://hvo.wr.usgs.gov/.

Although earthquakes can be disturbing, mudslides and drowning cause more loss of life and damage. Landslides and erosion, including especially beach erosion on Oahu and Maui, are also local geophenomena that raise concerns. Construction codes call for attention to such problems but heavy localized rainfall can cause sudden damage and flash flooding as in November 2000 on the Big Island.

Also, depending on the trade winds, you may experience vog, or volcanic fog. Vog is caused by emissions of the volcano. Though it only seriously affects people with chronic diseases such as emphysema and asthma, it contributes to health problems on the Big Island of Hawaii.

Temperate as it is, Hawaii is still not right for everyone. Recent fluctuations include above-average temperatures and dry spells bordering on drought conditions. These are regarded as effects of El Nino and La Nina in the Mid-Pacific. Some people find Hawaii too hot, too muggy and/or too wet. On the other hand, Robert Louis Stevenson, who suffered from tuberculosis, found Honolulu "too cold."

Consider also the economic climate of Hawaii. It runs hot and cold with periodic booms and busts, and has greater variations that the temperature. The economy of Hawaii has suffered a maelstrom of recession and economic dislocation, including a measure of out-migration, beginning in the early nineties. A succession of natural events, market conditions and politics have disrupted business, investment, and employment. The forced cutbacks and emergency measures have had an effect on virtually every segment of Hawaii's tourism and agricultural base. This has occurred as the Mainland forged ahead breaking records, setting new standards of success and in general, undergoing a prolonged period of prosperity while Hawaii teetered on the brink of collapse and even statewide bankruptcy through the decade of the 90s.

It is Hawaii's good fortune that Mainland-based investments, residents, and tourists sustained the ailing local economy through a decade of tough times. The population "trickle-in" occurred on all islands among older age groups, among them Mainland retirees.

Prospects for investment improved somewhat in the last two years of the 20th century, setting the stage for sustained recovery in the 21st century. However, if you are planning to retire in Hawaii be aware that the investment climate is still shaky, that the employment market is spotty at best and entry is often difficult for older workers. Many businesses have sought shelter in bankruptcy and many resident families hold multiple jobs in order to make ends meet. Despite that, there are signs in the real estate, retail, tourism and agriculture sectors that Hawaii's future will be brighter than the recent past. Despite the shaky job market, people with special skills in certain fields, such as medical personnel, airline mechanics and computer technicians, are in demand. Qualified teachers, social workers and nurses can find jobs on any island. Real estate prices, while still depressed, are creeping upward as new residents and young families unleash pent up demand. New housing starts are up and real estate brokers report a measure of renewed sales activity centered on Oahu but felt through the State.[xxviii] Recognizing a "boomlet," an industry spokesperson in the April 2000 issue of Hawaii Realtor Journal observed that Kona/Kohala on the Big Island, recently dubbed "Platinum Coast," had substantial increases in sales of homes and condominiums over last year. The bulk of these homes sold to "techno-rich" buyers from the west coast of the Mainland.[xxix]

In spite of the economic downturn, Hawaii can be a good place to invest—in agriculture and aquaculture, technology and communications, housing and real estate, leisure and recreation and even new wrinkles in tourism and entertainment. If you have extra investment dollars and do not risk your primary retirement income, you may wind up with income you did not anticipate. Beware of foreign markets, local regulations and red tape as well as the commonplace vagaries of business ventures. Business failures and bankruptcy have plagued Hawaii for a decade but the numbers are coming down.[xxx]

EMPLOYMENT

As the investment picture in Hawaii has improved employment prospects have followed suit, especially in the tourism and construction sectors with emerging opportunities in diversified agriculture and high tech occupations. If you, as many seniors do, intend to continue part or fulltime work be sure to update your resume, bring recommendation letters with you, and provide timely information in the application process. If you intend to pursue either agriculture or tourism as an entrepreneur be sure to allow time for your clientele and/or your crops to come to fruition (at least 3–5 years) before you intend to rely on the income. In any case, do not cut into your pension-retirement pie, which should be devoted to housing, healthcare and basic needs.

Immigrant and transplant seniors face the possibility of age discrimination as well as being labeled an "outsider". Local wages are somewhat depressed as compared with Mainland jobs and the cost of living in Hawaii can offset any increases that may accrue to you from experience or education. Also, labor unions are strong and dominate some lines of work. Ethnic favoritism is not uncommon and you may thus be regarded not only as an outsider but an outright interloper. Nonetheless, many seniors and retirees find suitable, even meaningful, employment as drivers, retail clerks, caterers and caretakers. Hopeful news for senior job seekers is found in *So You Want to Live in Hawaii.* "Resorts are beginning to seek middle-aged and retired people, because older people are more dependable and they don't take off when the surf is up."[xxxi] Others are gratified by the many volunteer opportunities present throughout the islands. Some retirees are able to maintain their careers or businesses (e.g. stock brokers, writers, website designers, etc.) via the modern miracles of communication. Others ply their trade in the islands with mixed results. Our best advice: have your pension, stock portfolio, or inheritance in hand before venturing to the Islands. If you are job hunting or starting a business allow for downtime, setbacks, and outright failure: don't gamble your hard won life savings on questionable enterprises; at the least hedge your bets and have a fall back position or contingency plan. For further information see www.hawaiijobs.com, and *So You Want to Live in Hawaii.*[xxxii]

KEEPING BUSY

What about mental and physical stimulation? A recent study for Rutgers University indicated that 75–80% of retirees would prefer to continue productive pursuits. i.e. starting a small business or part-time or modified employment. Few elected to retire forthwith with no objective or purpose or to pursue leisure and recreation as such. Hawaii offers many opportunities for cottage industry, i.e., arts, crafts, computer consultants, etc. Volunteer activities are widely available as well.

Ultimately, it is your personal equation of resources, tastes, age and anticipated income that will, or will not, make Hawaii an optimum choice for retirement. But before you make that decision, we urge you to weigh your options carefully, take in as much information as possible, and make several visits to the islands.

Chapter 2

Ethnic Relations and Population Trends

ETHNIC RELATIONS

If you suffer from xenophobia, commonly known as racism, Hawaii is probably not a wise retirement place for you. Oahu is the "Miami of the Pacific" with strands of <u>both</u> racial harmony and ethnic discord. The state itself, especially Oahu, with a resident population of just under one million, has a cosmopolitan demographic profile with an indigenous Hawaiian base.[xxxiii] But the ethnic demographics of Hawaii are far more complex and dynamic than most accounts allow, and the future for young and old alike will be no less so.[xxxiv]

The Native Hawaiians are a distinct minority in a population composed of eight identifiable ethnic groups and a myriad of sub-groups.[xxxv] The most prominent "national origins" other than Native or mixed Hawaiian heritage are: Caucasian (Euro-American), Japanese, Chinese, Filipino, Polynesian, Portuguese, and Spanish-Mexican. (See Table 2-1 for more detailed information.)

Recent immigration from Polynesia and Southeast Asia has added another demographic component to Hawaii's already complex ethnic profile. The South Pacific and Southeast Asian contingents are now going through the process of assimilation and upward mobility albeit from the lower rungs of the social ladder. This ethnic mix is unique to Hawaii and its history, especially the economic evolution from royal estate to agricultural lands and plantation estates to the dominance of military, high-rise hotels and tourism.

The annexation of Hawaii to the United States in 1898 signaled the pervasive presence of the *haole* group.[xxxvi] They (haoles) proliferated, invested and organized alongside the continuing influx of migrant workers. Various segments of in-migrant labor from Asia entered Hawaii's population and economy throughout he first half of the 20th century. The influx of Japanese money, if not families, in the decades of the 1970s and 1980s created a stir among the indigenous population and immigrants alike. Real estate prices soared, disrupting ownership and equity, and inflating real value.

The process of ethnic differentiation was capped in 1993 by the renewed efforts of the Native Hawaiian Sovereignty movement[xxxvii], which has intensified the awareness of differences. The "melting pot," although tarnished and cracked, continues to be the dominant metaphor for race relations in Hawaii. In his widely read book, *Hawaii Pono: A Social History*, Lawrence H. Fuchs remarks, "Hawaii is no longer an experiment in race relations or colonial administration. In the islands peoples of many races and cultures, largely only two or three generations from illiterate, peasant life, present the world's best example of dynamic social democracy."[xxxviii]

Inter-marriage among many ethnic groups is now commonplace as the melting pot brews a stew of Pacific Island cosmopolites. Communities and outer-island towns and villages retain an ethnic identity but overall there are heterogeneous mixtures found on every island. Each village, once a base for subsistence economy and/or plantation workers, is now racially mixed at virtually every age level. Although there are "clusters" of ethnic groupings, and "local" enclaves no neighborhood is entirely pure or exclusive. The only exception is the island of Niihau, which is privately owned by the non-Hawaiian Robinson family but reserved for 160 persons of Native Hawaiian ancestry.

The melting pot produces its own variations, a result of inter-marriage and assimilation. From this inter-marriage comes a separate group of poly-ethnic children. Veteran state statistician Robert Schmitt calculates that "approximately sixty percent of the children born in 1992 were the offspring of interracial unions. Membership in this *hapa*[xxxix] group will continue to grow, not only in size, but as a percentage of the entire population."[xl] As a group they will come to have considerable economic and political clout by 2020. They may eventually constitute an "ethnic" majority by 2050.

While ethnic conflict was latent and only occasionally expressed in the past, it intensified in the decade of the 90's with the overall decline in Hawaii's economy. This decline has contributed to dislocation, unemployment, drug abuse, domestic violence and foreclosures. It has also placed a strain on the welfare system. It has put a brake on foreign investment in land, housing and businesses formerly owned by local-born residents.

As Franklin Odo, former Director of University of Hawaii Ethnic Studies program, observed in 1992, "Race relations aren't as good as they used to be, and for them to improve we and our elected officials need to recognize this area as crucial to the future of Hawaii."[xli]

> Ethnic voting—more than any other factor—has defined the constituencies of Hawaii's Republican and Democratic parties since the territorial government began functioning in 1900...following statehood (1960), many held out the vision of a Hawaii in which the color of a person's skin and

the place of their origin would count for naught in Hawaii society or its politics...Three decades (1990s) later we see ethnicity playing an even larger role in the political equation.[xlii]

Ethnic discrimination in Hawaii is neither rampant nor subtle, but lies somewhere between. Job discrimination and housing discrimination are occasionally blatant. However, discrimination is checked by several conditions, including federal law and the fact that no single ethnic group exercises total domination in political and social issues. Each ethnic group interacts with the others in an ongoing series of compromises in which there is no permanent resolution and no terminus. Inter-marriage and family interaction continues to break down ethnic and racial barriers and results in a hybrid population in which no group is all-powerful.[xliii]

Most residents are rightly proud of the ethnic diversity that prevails throughout Hawaii. It has not always been so—"ethnic dominance" has passed through several hands in Hawaii's history.[xliv]

In the interest of presenting a fair and balanced view of the prospects for retirement and retirees in Hawaii one should bring into focus the sources and dynamics of the anti-_haole_ sentiment. Surprisingly it comes not only from Native Hawaiians and their supporters, but from Hoales who are themselves transplants from another time, place or culture. There were local residents we occasionally encountered who were opposed to the very research that makes up this book. The spirit of aloha, while widespread, is not universal.

In Hawaii one will encounter a "We got here first" mentality in several forms.[xlv] Curiously, these sentiments extend to Haoles of long-term residence and even newcomers. Newcomers are often regarded as latecomers or "outsiders" the propriety of whose presence is brought into question by those who preceded them and adopted Hawaii as home. Those who relocate without the proper attitude are somehow "tainted" by "American culture" or "Western values." Or, alternatively, an Oriental or Eastern mentality.

A minor county functionary went so far as to chastise the authors for writing "yet another book" extolling the islands and thus welcoming or beckoning to yet more newcomers. "It's already too crowded and too expensive [in Waimea]. Why add to the problem?" Why indeed!

The islands of Hawaii will do their own beckoning without and even in spite of our help. It's easy to overlook the obvious: "foreigners" have been coming to Hawaii and calling it and making it *home* for over 200 years, an extended right of passage that has profoundly and ineluctably shaped Hawaii this way and that.

The resulting heritage or culture, despite provincial Native Hawaiian claims, is as diverse as the many populations which contributed to it. The outcome is an international population and an interdependent economy fast leaving its plantation and territorial roots behind.

The Native Hawaiians are clearly restless on this point, depending on who one talks to with grudges of long standing dating back to 1778 and Captain Cook's voyage of "discovery" or the 1893 "overthrow" of the Hawaiian monarchy. But this provincialism does not stop there and is, in real terms, a factor in the insularity that characterizes parts of Hawaii's politics, culture, and economy. Many persons are affected by this, including the school age children who are woefully susceptible to misstatements of history.[xlvi]

Newcomers and transplants, most of whom even today bring their culture with them, should be forewarned: your <u>nouveau arrives</u> status which is too often regarded as that of an interloper intent on destroying the "traditions" or practices which are touted as older than the islands themselves. It is a culture trap set prior to the newcomers' presence, one that cannot be totally avoided but need not deter those who are informed and aware.[xlvii]

If you are going to live in Hawaii you are going to encounter people with skin pigment, physiological features, social history and cultural values different from your own. While it would be possible for you to withdraw into a closed circle of similar people, socializing with only your own kind, it means missing one of the great values of living in Hawaii—exposure to diverse ethnic groups and differing cultures.

Those of cosmopolitan mind and spirit, and those who celebrate diversity or who have suffered racial discrimination, will cherish Hawaii's rainbow mix of skin tones and features and attempt to extend and preserve it.

POPULATION TRENDS: THE TRICKLE-IN HYPOTHESIS

The population of Hawaii is over one million and increasing in average age. According to the 2000 census Hawaii's population rose from 1,108,229 in 1990 to 1,211,537, an increase of 9.3% over the ten years.

Hawaii's total population increase from 1950 through 1989 was more than one hundred percent. It leapt from 499,000 in 1950 to 1.1 million in 1989, an average increase of approximately two percent per year.[xlviii] These increases are traceable to two historical events: World War II (1941 to '45) and the admission of Hawaii as a state in 1959. This growth rate has slowed in recent years but is likely to rise again at a somewhat faster rate from 2000 to 2010. After that the population growth rate is expected to increase even faster: 2011 is when the baby-boom generation of 1946 to 1964 will begin to reach the nominal retirement age of sixty-five.

A significant proportion of this group will retire before age sixty-five but many will continue their employment beyond age seventy. During that ten-year period, 2000 to 2010, the influx of population to Hawaii could increase to as much as three percent per year. Our most sober estimate is that the current rate of increase hovers about 2%, possibly more, and will increase 2.8% to 3.2% by 2010 with unpredictable increases after that point. This would increase Hawaii's total population to more than two million residents by 2020, possibly three million by 2030. Some scenarios mark the growth at an even faster rate based on reduced outward-migration and a modest increase in average family size. Hawaii could, therefore, be home to three million people in just thirty years.

Interestingly, the over-sixty-five population is expected to grow even faster than the total population. The *Hawaii Summit: 2011 Project*, completed in 1998, summarizes the work done by the Office on Aging and focuses on the "demographic revolution occurring in Hawaii." The summation contends "between 2000 and 2010, the sixty-plus group is projected to grow by seventy-two percent to 299,500 persons, while the eighty-five-plus group will grow by two hundred and eighty-six percent to 40,120 persons. In contrast, the total population will increase by only twenty-nine percent over the same period."[xlix]

Not all population figure projections agree with this substantial rate of increase. According to State of Hawaii figures, during that ten-year period, the state will experience a <u>slowing</u> of population growth to approximately one percent increase per year. The Department of Business, Economic Development and Tourism (DBEDT) claims that "the growth rates of both the resident and de facto [including military and tourist components] populations are expected to be lower from 1995 to 2020 than they were between 1980 and 1995."[l]

Note that projected figures for 2010 by DBEDT are at variance with U.S. Census figures, a difference of some 183,000 people. DBEDT experts project a slower increase of population based on assumptions about economic development, especially the creation of new jobs for the existing work force.[li]

Both of these projections (U.S. Census and DBEDT) may be misleading. State demographic experts, while aware of the "paradise tax" and "tax hell"[lii] aspects of Hawaii's economy, may have overlooked or depressed the effect of the "sunshine and leisure" factors on Hawaii's population growth as well as the population movement in the U.S. from Northeast to Southwest, especially California. We contend they have tended to underestimate the lure of Hawaii to Mainland residents and persons of wealth the world over.

The official projections may also have underestimated the effects of 1) global and regional migration, 2) in-migration increases in the number of legal and illegal aliens, and 3) population growth on the Mainland where increases have created an impetus to "move on" among certain age and economic groups. These groups usually include those over fifty-five with an annual income of sixty to eighty thousand dollars. While seemingly sound, official projections tend to underestimate immigration to Hawaii, especially of retirees and "young" seniors — those fifty-five and up. Out-migration will continue, especially if jobs in Hawaii are scarce, while Mainland employment figures are up and jobs are plentiful.

A correction will occur based on the results of the 2000 Census, which officially recognizes a tendency to undercount the resident population. We have already witnessed the increasing number of retirees relocating to Hawaii. That trend will continue, though future retirees will not come in droves or hordes. The most likely scenario is a relatively steady "trickle-in" increasing as Baby Boomers approach retirement age. The influx could run as high as one hundred thousand per year (total population) between 2020 and 2030.

Large numbers of seniors relocating to Hawaii in years to come will have an impact on the state demographically, economically and socially. If the net "trickle-in" is only one percent per year, there will be even more dramatic shifts in average age. The impact of retirees could be comparable to the impact of sugar plantation workers, whaling industry, military personnel and tourists in decades past. Retirees are likely to be the "next wave" of population with the potential to change the course of Hawaii's future.

One effect would be a shift of ethnic composition. If the immigration is predominantly Euro-American from the U.S. Mainland, a major ethnic and realignment of political forces in Hawaii is possible. Euro-Americans now constitute twenty-five to thirty percent of the total population, and that percentage appears to be increasing.[liii] With local-born residents leaving Hawaii, over time the Euro-American group could become the dominant ethnic group with an effective political majority (40% +) by 2020 to 2030. This has not been seen since Native Hawaiians once dominated the legislature during the first 50 years of territorial government.[liv]

Retirees en masse will additionally bring an increased demand for a wide range of goods and services. Where they choose to live is especially important, and could dramatically alter the face of Hawaii. State services and Federal funding could face potential disruptions and shortfalls because of inadequate planning.

On the political front, retirees will carry their voting power with them to Hawaii. In future elections the silver set will be a strong force.[lv] The over-fifty-five group is likely to register to vote in increasing numbers as younger voters and citizens remain disenchanted. One of the AARP (formerly American Association of Retired Persons) primary objectives is to organize older voters into a voting bloc and give expression to their priorities and needs.[lvi]

Young or early retirees are already present in Hawaii. In their mid-forties to late-fifties they take early retirement and set their sights on Hawaii. This "early retirement" group or phased, i.e., "preemies" (premature retirees), includes musicians and artists, scientists and technicians, civil servants and military personnel. It includes people of wealth and people on welfare. They bring assets with them, and, age aside, they bring skills and talents that will shape and contribute to the economy and culture of Hawaii. They have emerged as a political, economic, and cultural force to be reckoned with, a force on the rise in numbers, dollars, and votes.

And the early retirement group is not alone. Many people of standard retirement age have chosen Hawaii as well. This influx is likely to continue. Many couples will choose Hawaii for semi-retirement or intermittent retirement where one person retires or pursues retirement activity while a spouse or partner continues conventional employment. Others will come seeking respite or recovery from accident or illness, perhaps to stay, perhaps to return to familiar circumstances upon recovery. For some of these Hawaii will constitute a hospice environment—a good place to die—rather than an exclusively residential site.[lvii]

The recent decade of population increases will have short and long term fallout with major impacts on resources. Adding to this are shifting ethnic and racial patterns that will create new alliances and new allegiances throughout the state.

Hawaii's total population in the 2000 census exceeded 1.2 million, a deceptively modest 9.3% increase over 1990.[lviii] But that only begins to tell a story of an evolving population with a possibly dramatic and even calamitous future. The key figures are the 20% + populations gains on the "outer islands which are not likely to remain either "outer" or rural very long. Add to these increases the average daily number of tourists and transients along with the extended vacationers, second and third home owners, seasonal retirees and transplant newcomers of all ages and you have a not a brain drain or an ebb in population, but a new demographic profile with new and profound political, economic and cultural prospects. For every lost job and school closing there will be three or four new residents demanding and thus creating one or two new service jobs. New voting patterns will emerge. New businesses serving older populations will follow.

Population increases in the outer islands pose an opportunity for transplants, Mainland retirees and immigrants alike and constitute a problem for Hawaii's extant and established population fluid and diverse as it is. [lix] It is an opportunity for the incoming population to generate a new strain of island culture and a new level of assimilation and integration; it is a problem for Hawaii to sustain the traditional communities and the rural lifestyle, that much-touted "laid back" atmosphere, and the attitudes which attend it.

Are these trends truly antithetical? Can Kamaaina (resident) and the perpetual stream of malihinis (newcomers) survive each other? Can newcomer and established residents co-exist without an endless we-got-here-first debate? Can the Native Hawaiians and the tourists who are potential residents do more than gawk at one another? Whose interests will prevail? Whose chicken will be singed?

How will population increases affect the roughly 350 thousand persons living on the rural islands of Kauai, Maui, and Hawaii, parts of which (Kona and Maui South Shore) are already clearly gentrified? Lanai presents a clear-cut example. Small, undeveloped, and lightly populated it is undergoing such a transformation. The '90's saw an increase in population of 31.6% (from 2426 to 3193) suggesting that Lanai is about to undergo the transition from plantation economy to a tourist and real estate development project not unlike South Shore Maui and the Kona Coast.[lx] The land mass that was once the province of Dole pineapple fields is about to be upscaled as no island before it, that is, gentrified, developed, bulldozed, and landscaped for the very well to do with their equipage and entourage in tow. This has and will create jobs to be sure but at a radical cost of ultra modernization superimposed on a previously agricultural population and economy.

A 9.3% statewide increase in resident population can be managed as can a 4.8 % net increase on Oahu as it approaches the mythic one million limit.[lxi] While crowding and congestion plague the "Gathering Place", it is the rural islands where the transformations will occur in their most visible and palpable form.[lxii] Retiring to "outer islands" will become less and less a bargain as crowding occurs and tax burdens are shifted to pay for aging or non-existent infrastructure. However, as of 2000 the rural islands are still a good buy and a good bet for residing or investing. For one thing, they are still rural, i.e. uncrowded, especially Kauai and Hawaii. By 2010 to 2020 this "rurality" could be history, an endangered species in its own right.

These impacts are already being felt on Maui and the Big Isle where the gains over 1990 population were 23.6% and 27.6% respectively. Rural Oahu is a fading relic as urbanization swells from a creep to a gallop. Kauai and Molokai will follow in time precisely because of their remoteness and seclusion.

As these trends continue during the next thirty years, Hawaii's population has the potential to shift dramatically. If this occurs, retirees—headed to the islands in increasing numbers—will constitute a major force in the 50th state. Considering other factors we may bear witness to a completely altered Hawaiian society, built around a core of mixed ethnic groups and a cosmopolitan population. This assimilation process is likely to yield a "mixed plate," a state without a specific ethnic identification.

Chapter 3

The Islands

The State of Hawaii has four centers of government. 1) The City and County of Honolulu is the governing body of the entire island of Oahu and is lead by an elected mayor and county council. Each county has an elected mayor, county council, county charter and county plan. Honolulu is also the state capitol (the governor and state legislature have offices in Honolulu) and Honolulu is home to most Federal offices as well. 2) The County of Hawaii is the island of Hawaii. 3) The County of Maui includes the islands of Maui, Lanai and Molokai. 4) The islands of Kauai and Niihau constitute the County of Kauai. With the exception of Honolulu there are no cities or townships as they are known on the Mainland. For an excellent treatment of government see *Land and Power*.[lxiii]

OAHU: THE URBAN CENTER

Most people never get further than Oahu on their visits to Hawaii. For tourists and residents alike Honolulu is a fast-paced city, and Oahu, known traditionally as The Gathering Place, is a decidedly urbanized island. Its growing population of about one million is crowded onto an island of six hundred and eight square miles, much of which is not habitable. Residential or commercial real estate is a mere 5 - 10% of the island's surface, but parts of Honolulu are among the most densely populated in the world.[lxiv]

Most of the island serves as a suburb to Honolulu, the center of government and commerce. Areas such as Waimanalo, Ewa Beach, Pearl City and the windward "suburbs" of Kaneohe and Kailua are made accessible by Oahu's interstate highway system, a clogged and sorry rush-hour mess. In The Honolulu Advertiser January 2000 Susan Hooper reported that "the (traffic) tie-ups and costs on Oahu are likely to get worse before they get better."[lxv] There are relatively remote areas with light traffic, such as Waialua, Makaha and Haleiwa. Yet the size of Oahu, roughly forty-four by forty-eight miles, puts everyone within commuting distance of Honolulu proper. A bus system serves the entire island and is available to tourists and residents alike.

Much controversy surrounds the contemporary version of Honolulu. Many pine for a not too distant past with chummy bars, truly local talent, beach boys and hula girls galore, the pre-WWII incarnation of Hawaii. Others want to render virtually the entire city and island a "cultural landmark" or a "historical site" just to make sure the tourists still come there. Most residents just want a clean, affordable city with less traffic, lower taxes and better schools, the warp and woof of the American middle class.

Honolulu was once called the "Cesspit of the Pacific,"[lxvi] an overbuilt, overpriced, oversold place that provides jobs in order to make ends meet in Hawaii. The "brain drain" of the 90's, while slowed, is still a problem for the local economy. In the course of providing employment and the means of commerce, an entire island, has been urbanized to a point of dangerous density posing a threat to those very jobs and that commerce by overburdening the environment and depleting its resources. As one astute commentator put it "Honolulu dominates the urban hierarchy of the state" and sustains over 75 percent of the state's population.[lxvii]

Honolulu is regarded as a "metropolis" and most of the build-able land on Oahu has been so utilized with an astonishing degree of density, especially in Waikiki which is regarded as "crowded, commercial, noisy and tawdry." [lxviii]

The entire island of Oahu, beautiful and bountiful as it is, is threatened, especially its more remote areas where the "available acreage is diminishing rapidly."[lxix] Plans are underway to both preserve and refurbish various parts of the city and county of Honolulu, but again at an astonishing cost not the least of which is the loss of the very charm, romance and sense of remoteness sought by tourist, resident and native alike.

Many retirees, including those born, bred and employed on Oahu, have turned away from this image and all too ugly reality as it bears on the future of this urban metroplex and its tourist ambience. Others, including Mainlanders, early retirees, and those who thrive on the offerings of upscale urbanism will embrace it to the tune of millions of dollars for housing and equipage of the upper classes.

People seriously considering a move to Waikiki are advised to consult the following sources available from the Planning Department of the City and County of Honolulu:

1. *Restoring Hawaiianness to Waikiki*, George S. Kanahele, The Queen Emma Foundation, 1994

2. *Waikiki Master Plan, 1992* Department of General Planning, City and County of Honolulu

3. *Living in Waikiki*, a report on interviews with 48 Waikiki residents, The Planning Department, City and County of Honolulu, Dinell, Tom, assisted by Karl Kim, Professor of Urban and Regional Planning, University of Hawaii, 1997.

The major segment of the older adult population resides in the city of Honolulu. In 1980, approximately 84,000 older adults lived on Oahu. By 1990, the Oahu elderly population had increased to 128,490, representing 15.4 percent of the total population.[lxx] By 2000 that number is expected to be 150,000 or more. [see Office on Aging and U.S. Census, also DBEDT]. Many older adults reside in the districts of Honolulu, Ewa, and Koolaupoko.

Oahu's elders are active and growing in numbers. This can be attributed to the island's bountiful array of services, from food to health care. The city of Honolulu offers most big-city amenities - theater, symphony, sporting events, shopping malls, hospitals, senior centers, nursing homes, hospice centers, mass transit and many parks and public attractions.

Sophisticated and lively, Oahu is the only island with "interstate" highways that do not go to another state. It boasts an abundance of galleries, nightclubs, and museums, a major zoo, an aquarium, Iolani Palace (the only royal palace on U.S. soil), Pearl Harbor, the Arizona memorial, and much more.[lxxi]

UNIVERSITY OF HAWAII

On Oahu, the University of Hawaii is available to seniors and retirees as a resource for students of all ages. Located in Manoa Valley, the campus has grown to dominate the lower valley and adjacent hills. UH is a well-regarded, up-to-date state university with an urban student body of just over seventeen thousand. The campus features five libraries, the East-West Cultural Exchange Center, sport fields, and the arresting architecture and charming floral beauty that is so characteristically Hawaiian. The scent of plumeria is often present across the campus in the morning hours.

Seniors have numerous privileges, and may take coursework at a discount fee, seek out on-campus entertainment, including music, theater and dance, as well as browse the bookstores and coffee shops of lower Manoa Valley.

The campus is crowded and parking is typically maddening. However access is readily available from all parts of Honolulu via public transit, taxi and tour bus. The campus is, with a few exceptions, accessible to disabled and elderly persons.

A multi-campus community college system (with an enrollment of over 44,000 and campuses and course offerings on all islands[lxxii]) supports and extends the University, providing affordable course work in vocational and technical fields, as well as Hawaiian studies. Their libraries and the statewide public systems are invaluable sources of information, and are highly utilized. Hawaii and the University of Hawaii are well placed for the emerging distance-learning trend. The university sports program is first class for men and women alike.

HOUSING

Apartments are available from about six hundred dollars per month up to two thousand per month for a one-bedroom apartment (unfurnished) in one of the many mid-priced areas surrounding Honolulu, such as Makiki, Kaimuki and Punchbowl. For view and resort-area apartments add twenty to thirty percent. Studios may be rented on a weekly or monthly basis for as low as two hundred dollars per week for a partly furnished unit; in the Waikiki area that figure will double or triple.

OAHU: REAL ESTATE

The real estate scene on Oahu, and especially Honolulu, is a one-of-a-kind, exceptionally volatile, and unusually structured market, subject to booms, busts and all shades betwixt and between.

Residential housing is subject to huge variations in price and value, and is almost constantly in short supply for middle-income buyers. The housing market is also subject to a variety of legal and environmental restrictions that make a "cold purchase," or owners-only negotiation, a questionable alternative. Financing in Hawaii is also problematic, since buyers must establish residency and credit, and meet other criteria, pursuant to purchase. Fraud and bilking are sometimes present but not always detectable as transactions occur.[lxxiii] New residents should ask questions, take their time, seek second opinions and legal advice, and orient themselves not only to market conditions but to the environment and the potential vagaries of the City and County of Honolulu. To fail to do so invites a waste of time and money, and can completely disrupt an otherwise satisfactory retirement.

Except for the golf aficionados, and the overkill effort to promote condominiums on Maui and Oahu in the 1980s and 90s, much of the retirement market remains untapped and unappreciated. Not many developers are targeting the middle-income retiree, but a few have read the signals, and are preparing for the influx, be it a trickle or a tidal wave of moderately affluent, well-educated seniors in the 55 to 75 age group.

A perusal of local sources shows a clear trend toward recovery of both the overall Island economy and the real estate and construction industries, especially on Oahu and the Kona coast of the Big Island. Hawaii Real Estate Indicators, a local quarterly real estate report published by Prudential Locations in Honolulu, observes that, "Hawaii appears to be in the early stages of a residential construction cycle."[lxxiv] A dearth of new housing has been a source of pressure on the resale markets of all islands. In the first quarter of 2000, the condominium resale market was "very strong."[lxxv] This is particularly true for the neighbor [rural] islands where sales are at a higher annual rate than the boom period of 10 years ago. The Oahu condominium market is also at a sales rate last seen in 1990.[lxxvi]

The Oahu condominium market is constrained by the ever-present "leasehold situation" but fee simple resales are running at their highest rate ever.[lxxvii]

Residential resale market prices have increased sharply in the high-ticket neighborhoods of Waialae, Kahala, and Hawaii Kai; specific areas on the windward shores, such as Lanikai and Kailua Beach, have seen price increases of 20 to 25 percent in this year alone. This rush of sales and lack of new starts is rapidly depleting the existing stock of residential and condominium units, thus portending sharper increases in sale prices, unless and until the construction industry responds.

Many projects on the table in the 1990s are still on hold as buyers and investors sober up from the decade-long slump. Several projects on each island were canceled or suffered bankruptcy in the 1990s. With only a few viable projects on the drawing boards, and the stock of available housing dwindling, "there is little to suggest this situation will change anytime soon."[lxxviii] The buyer's market of the 1990s is evolving into a seller's dream as the new millennium begins. Clearly, bargains are still available on Oahu, as elsewhere, but prices will surely rise as the cost of new construction and new materials take effect, and as the influx of residents, including retirees, renders demand more resilient.

WATER SUPPLY

One problem that plagues Honolulu, most of Oahu and indeed, all of Hawaii, is an adequate supply of drinking water. Water quality and the supply of fresh water is both a conservation and a development issue: conservation because there is not always an adequate supply due to local droughts and arid periods, development because the demands of the future appear to exceed the projected supply. In some areas, such as Manoa Valley, water is almost always excessive; in other regions, like leeward areas of

Molokai and the Big Island, water is always in short supply, and always expensive.[lxxix]

Disputes over water supply in Hawaii are legion and have a long history in the courts.

Oahu, with its massive population, faces the most severe problems in the 21st Century. An adequate water supply could be <u>the</u> factor that limits population growth, agricultural production and economic development.

New technologies and conservation measures may ameliorate and forestall the problem. But the fact remains that in some areas and at some times, there will not be enough potable water to go around. In Honolulu, this is projected to be part of a four billion dollar infrastructure problem in the coming decades, intended to restore and extend water mains, upgrade deep production wells, and improve runoff drains. This could be a terrible burden on the residents and taxpayers of Oahu.

Local spot shortages occur with some frequency on the rural islands, necessitating truck transport of water for drinking and agricultural purposes. Check the water tables, production capacity and future plans prior to relocating.[lxxx] Catchment systems are commonplace in the mountainous areas of Oahu and on the rural islands. Desalination projects and deep wells are underway, but there is no way to guarantee an increase in rainfall as abundant as it is in some areas. In rural areas on all islands, many residents utilize simple rainwater catchment systems, coupled with bottled water for drinking and cooking. Contamination can be a serious public health problem, especially for those aging persons with gastro-intestinal problems.

Unless radical steps are taken, and a few have been, Oahu may become an island-wide megalopolis with only mountain ranges and water resources spared. The entire island may become paved and wired, with underclass pockets of slums and blights with areas of upscale development literally adjacent to what used to be rural. In future decades the result will be a spillover, especially among local retirees, to the neighbor islands. This process began more than a decade ago and the trend is well under way.

Lest we be misunderstood, allow us to add that Oahu is blessed with many beautiful sights and picturesque beaches - witness Haunauma Bay, Waimanalo Beach, Kailua Beach Park or Ala Moana Beach Park where children and adults of all ages spend endless hours in the sun and surf. However, be prepared to share them with others – many others - especially on sunny weekend days, when Oahu's million plus residents will be seeking the same sun and surf en masse.[lxxxi]

Toni Polancy, author of *So You Want to Live in Hawaii*, observed that the best thing about Oahu is that there is a multitude of events, festivals and celebrations. She viewed Oahu's worst characteristics as traffic congestion and crowding, a sentiment echoed by many residents.[lxxxii] We agree. Any place where the morning news is dominated by traffic tie-ups and the evening news by the day's crime is not high on our list of places to retire. On the other hand, violent crimes in Hawaii are the exception with crime numbers down for the past three years. Unfortunately, tourist robberies and attacks receive a disproportionate amount of media coverage. The majority of crime in the islands involves driving under the influence (DUI), domestic violence and marijuana possession/cultivation.

TRANSPORTATION

It is possible to live comfortably in Honolulu utilizing only public transit. For those who do not drive, the City and County of Honolulu transportation on Oahu provides reliable service covering the entire island. TheBus is the municipal transit system. Senior citizens sixty-five and over may purchase a two-year pass for twenty dollars. Regular adult one-way fare is one dollar. Visitors may buy a four-day pass for ten dollars. Buses run on a regular schedule from ten to twenty-five minutes apart. TheBus is online at www.thebus.org, or call 808-848-5555. Instituted by former Mayor Frank Fasi in the 1960s, TheBus has become a much relied upon institution for students, laborers, residents and tourists alike. Elder/disabled transportation options are available. Call the Office on Aging for information. Although there are bus and transit systems on other islands, they are sometimes irregular and unreliable.

We were tempted to write off Oahu as being overcrowded, overpriced, and overbearing with its hyped tourism and artificial culture. Still, Honolulu is a happening town and Oahu has not only beautiful beaches but other natural attractions and amenities as well that make it a highly desirable urban retirement site. In those respects Honolulu is not unlike Las Vegas, San Diego, Phoenix, Fort Meyers in Florida and Corpus Christi in Texas.

As a student in the 60s and as tourists in the 70s and extended visitors in the 80s we experienced what we regard as the best and worst of Oahu, of Honolulu, and of Waikiki. We suffered delayed flights, traffic snarls, poor service, high prices, and social and environmental problems as we came to view Hawaii from various perspectives over the years.

On a recent field trip to Oahu, we took another look at the North Shore. (See Chapter Eight: Fruits of Our Labors). In contrast to the bustling, city life of Honolulu, we found open space, fabulous beaches, and green lush landscapes. It is still rural with roadside stands selling fruit, kids carrying their surfboards and miles of farmland between villages.

If you choose Oahu as your retirement spot, we recommend a preliminary rental of six months to as long as two years. Rent an apartment or condominium and allow yourself time to search for a permanent home. If you are still on Oahu after two years, it is indicative of your tolerance for urban life under the sun. If you're driven out or scared off by high prices, crowds, malls and traffic you may be ready to sample the neighbor islands with relish and a sense of relief.

HAWAII: THE BIG ISLAND

A garland of coastal villages ring the island of Hawaii, augmented by upland settlements, relics of the plantation[lxxxiii] and paniolo[lxxxiv] eras creating a rural motif ideally suited to retirement living. Residents involved in recent economic development planning meetings have expressed the desire to retain the village setting and open spaces along the coast as well as the mountainous areas. They want new jobs, but hope that the vagaries of economic development won't reach their doorstep. The island of Hawaii is especially receptive to newcomers and seniors with a "Welcome wagon" that visits new residents with information, coupons, calendars, and a smile. The Big Island of Hawaii was our choice and we highly recommend it.[lxxxv]

Of all the islands, Hawaii is the largest of the chain at 4,028 square miles. Hawaii, also known as the Orchid Isle, has the most diversified climates and environment. Only on Hawaii is it possible to snow ski in the morning and surf in the afternoon. The Hawaii Visitors and Convention Bureau, Hawaii Island Chapter publishes a brochure calling the Big Island "The Golf Capital of Hawaii." It describes fourteen courses; some designed by world-class golf course designers Robert Trent Jones, Jr. and Robert Trent Jones, Sr. Visiting golfers, resident golfers and golf events keep these clubs busy throughout the year.

The geography on the island is dominated by two volcanoes. Mauna Kea, a thirteen thousand foot volcanic mountain, is the premier site for worldwide astronomy research, and Volcanoes

National Park, a center for vulcanology and geology also features Kilauea a still active volcano and popular tourist attraction.[lxxxvi] Some areas in volcanic rift zones appear buildable and habitable but may be uninsurable, because many homes have been covered by lava. A black sand beach (Kalapana) was completely covered by lava in the Puna District in 1984. As previously mentioned, vog, a combination of volcanic gases and fog, can be a problem for those with respiratory problems. From time to time it plagues the west and southwest portion of the island. Nonetheless, many parcels, older homes, and small farms are available and affordable in the remote Puna and Ka'u regions.

ECONOMY OF THE BIG ISLAND

The County of Hawaii has keenly felt the recession in spite of the overall growth in tourism. Investors and retirees are reporting a "buyer's market." Some foresee a sustained turnaround on the island of Hawaii based on falling prices locally and rising demand for housing. J.W.A. Buyers, chairman and chief executive officer of C. Brewer and Co., Ltd, remarked that "the outlook for continued low interest rates and economic growth for the country will enable us to build a huge wave of interest in relocation to the island of Hawaii."[lxxxvii] C. Brewer moved its corporate headquarters to Hilo in 1998 anticipating a boomlet as well as long-term growth. In October of 1999 the *Hawaii Tribune-Herald* reported that "housing is cheaper on the Big Island than on Oahu, another possible reason more Mainland transplants and Honolulu 'refugees' prefer the Big Island."[lxxxviii]

The island of Hawaii also provides the widest range of prices for housing and real estate available anywhere in the islands. Homes in Hilo and elsewhere start as low as sixty thousand dollars. Rural lots and parcels are available for as little as five to ten thousand dollars. These building sites may not have electricity, county water or paved roads.

In 1990, just over 20,000 individuals sixty years of age and older resided on the Big Island of Hawaii. This population represented about seventeen percent of the total island population (120,317).[lxxxix] Most of these individuals were residing in the South Hilo area. South Hilo includes Hilo Town and the coastal area north of Hilo to Papaikou (approximately 11 miles).

The Hawaii Island population will be the first to double into as many as three hundred thousand by 2030. The population will become older, wealthier and more cosmopolitan than ever. Hawaii Island, and to a lesser extent Maui, will become a playground for persons of wealth and leisure creating their own measure of insularity in resort-style living.

KONA, WAIMEA, HILO AND PUNA

Hawaii is served by three commercial centers – Kona, Waimea and Hilo. Like the other islands, Hawaii has a windward and leeward side. The Kona Coast (home of world famous Kona coffee) is the leeward and dry side of the island—the tourist center for deep sea fishing, snorkeling, luxury resorts, boutiques, art shops and fabulous sunsets. An increasing segment of the tourist population spend their vacations here. However, it is expensive, and has become known as "the gold coast" in reference especially to its opulent resorts, high price ocean front property and gilded lifestyle.

Waimea[xc] (also called Kamuela) is located in the north central uplands of what used to be the cowboy, or *paniolo* country of the Island. Parker Ranch and other smaller ranches still keep cattle on thousands of acres. The area is at about 2500-3500 feet elevation and cooler than sea level. It remains popular and attractive to immigrants from Seattle and Canada. Upscale subdivisions and new housing starts are visible throughout the area in the two-to five hundred thousand dollar market. Older homes sell within these price ranges as well.

Hilo is on the "wet" or windward side and is known for its orchids, macadamia nut farms, fishing and lush gardens. Average annual rainfall at Hilo Airport is 128 inches. (See Table 1-4.) Hilo is the county seat and the largest population center on the Big Island, with about forty-six thousand people. The University of Hawaii at Hilo campus founded in 1974 is home to twenty-seven hundred students and sponsors a senior lecture series. The Hawaii Community College and Hilo Adult School offer low cost courses of interest to the many active seniors in Hilo.

Puna District, south of Hilo, is home to a diverse group of retirees, many of whom opt for the modestly priced one-to-five-acre parcels located in large partially developed subdivisions. Many orchid farms and nurseries are found in the Puna district.

CANNABIS

The Puna area of the Big Island, Molokai, and the more remote parts of Kauai are notorious for marijuana cultivation by growers who on occasion have been known to guard their crops with guns and booby traps. Some dealers steal from each other and this can provoke further confrontations. Sometimes "hard drugs" (meth-amphetamines, "crack," cocaine and psychedelics) are involved. Therefore, as in many Mainland cities, some neighborhoods are rendered undesirable because of these criminal activities.

Partly as a result of the Federal marijuana eradication program, the price of cannabis is at an all time high. In fact, marijuana production has been a major part of Hawaii's 'underground" economy for the last 20 years or more. The Federally sponsored eradication program has other fallout. Many residents living near targeted areas complain of the low flying helicopters scaring animals and children, and disturbing sleep. This situation is likely to continue, so long as the "war on drugs" continues as national policy.

TRANSPORTATION

Various options are available to those who prefer to live without a car. The HeleOn Bus runs from Kona to Hilo and back on regular schedules. However, most of the routes are for the convenience of hotel workers going to and returning from Kona. Bus tickets offer riders a 10 percent discount off the regular fare rate. Certified senior citizens (60 and over), disabled persons and students are entitled to and save 33-1/3 percent off the regular fare. Monthly passes are available as well.

In addition to bus service, the County of Hawaii offers a flexible shared-ride taxi service. For as little as $2, obtain door-to-door transportation service anywhere within the residential and commercial areas of Hilo and Kona. Taxi and bus schedule information: 808-961-8744. The Hele On Bus can also be a bargain tour of the island in contrast to $150 circle island tour buses where your bladder must conform to their time-table.

MAUI: THE VALLEY ISLE

Some will find much of Maui too upscale and too developed for the retiree of modest means. Maui was home to the first resort in Hawaii outside Waikiki. Since then, Maui has become the most visited rural island, with activity concentrated on the West Coast. Maui was a major sugar production center until the last decade when tourism pulled ahead as the dominant industry. The island is ringed by forty-two miles of world-famous exquisite beaches, resort developments and shopping centers. The beaches range from the little red sand beach to the striking black sand beach at Waianapanapa State Park.

The higher elevations of each island are locally referred to as "upcountry" or mauka.[xci] In the case of Maui, upcountry refers to the slopes of Haleakala. Upcountry hosts ranching and quiet country living. The green pastures and sweeping vistas remind one of rangeland in Wyoming. And Makawao town provides a taste of the "old west." Paia is also an old cowboy town popular with visitors, outdoor enthusiasts and old timers. Paia lies on the famous winding road to Hana with its fifty-three bridges, some of them in need of extensive repair.[xcii]

In beautiful, serene and secluded Hana, you'll discover a Hawaii similar to the one before World War II, statehood and tourism. Hana is quaint, remote and very local. Ray Reigert in *Hidden Hawaii* adds, "This Eden-like town... Known as "heavenly Hana," is a ranch town inhabited primarily by part-Hawaiians. Because of its remote location it has changed little over the years."

In west Maui, Kihei is a developed residential area with homes, condominiums, dining and beachfront living. Canadian and American "snowbirds" vacation in and own homes and condominiums in this area.

Lahaina, once a whaling center, is now a bustling tourist area offering historic sites, ocean activities (fishing, sailing, snorkeling, wind surfing) and shopping. Today, much of the town is a national landmark. Amidst thirty restored historic sites, you'll find a mix of art galleries, restaurants and clubs. Although Lahaina is the center of Maui's nightlife, there are great restaurants all around the island. Many feature Hawaiian regional cuisine, one of the most celebrated cuisines in the world.

Some observers and long-time residents view the town as too glitzy, upscale and expensive. As one observer remarked, "Lahaina is beginning to look more like Sausalito (California) than Sausalito." The whole town gives the impression of a theme mall, made over for tourists and moviemakers. Just north of Lahaina, Kaanapali is a resort area built around a golf course. There are resorts, shopping, condominiums, and single family homes in the half million and up range.

In 1990, approximately 16,000 older adults resided in Maui County. This sixty-plus population represents fifteen point five percent of the total county population of 100,374. More than half of these adults were residing in the Wailuku area.[xciii] The Kahuli/Wailuku area, the state and county seat, is home also to the island's biggest shopping mall, airport and hospitals.

A substantial network of retiree communities may be found throughout the island with retirement centers in Kihei, Lahaina, Wailuku and Paia. Senior residence hotels have arrived and offer rental living with every level of service available—at a price. Medical services are available at hospitals, clinics and medical offices. However, limited access to some services and specialists force many patients to seek medical care such as surgery in Honolulu. For seniors who need greater assistance, adult residential care homes, adult day care and assisted-living facilities provide these services on Maui (see Chapter 5, Health for additional discussion).

HOUSING PRICES

Low-income housing programs assist the economically challenged. There are condominiums available from eighty to one hundred thousand dollars. Additionally, many buildings are aging and in disrepair. This means there are "fixers" available to those who can do-it-themselves.

A sampling of average sales prices on Maui as of January 31, 2000 are as follows (Source, Maui Board of Realtors):

Central:
Single family, $311,261
Condominium, $114,750
Kaanapali:
Single family, $853,333
Condominium, $414,600
Kihei:
Single family, $265,445
Condominium, $156,375
Lahaina
Single family, $245,000
Condominium, $466,500
Makawao:
Single family, $285,214

As for recreation, Maui has plenty. For the nature enthusiast, Maui's breathtaking hiking trails beckon. The Hawaii Nature Center in Iao Valley is a good starting place. The rangers at Haleakala National Park lead free nature walks, both at the ten thousand foot summit of Maui's awe-inspiring, long-dormant volcano, and at Oheo gulch with its famous seven pools. For the really adventurous senior you can take a harrowing bicycle ride down a treacherous hill.

Maui is also home to Maui Arts and Cultural Center, which brings concerts, lectures and performances from Oahu, the Mainland and beyond. Maui Community College is another bountiful source of life long learning, theater, music and sports events.

TRANSPORTATION

Transportation services for the elderly (60 years and over) are provided by Maui Economic Opportunity Council (MEO) and Kaunoa Senior Services. Public shuttle services with predetermined routes and rural shuttle services are available as well as assisted transportation for frail, isolated elderly who are unable to board buses. For more information, contact MEO Transportation Section on Maui at 877-7651.

The pricey resorts on Maui make it an expensive place to call home (everyone pays the same price for gas). Nonetheless the beauty of the island coupled with the comforts of modern amenities and a sizable retirement community can make this lush island, with its erstwhile rural ambiance, a preferred retirement site.

KAUAI: THE GARDEN ISLE

"The Garden Island," as it is known locally, is a picture-postcard tropical paradise blessed with a mild climate, wide sand beaches and waterfall-etched mountains. Kauai's ruggedness and remoteness bespeak romance, and adventure, even intrigue, making it an ideal backdrop for motion pictures like South Pacific, Temple of Doom and Jurassic Park. This theme is reiterated in the river cruises (Kauai has six navigable rivers), fern grotto, and other theme tours, including the movie sites themselves.

Kauai's resident population in 1998 was 56,603 on a landmass of five hundred and fifty-two square miles. Only twenty percent smaller than Oahu, Kauai's population is less than one-tenth that of Oahu. This yields a population density of just over 100 per square mile, a figure far below Oahu's density of 1,400 per square mile. The population on Oahu is thus 14 times as dense as Kauai. The uncrowded, quiet, slower feeling is what attracts residents and returning visitors to Kauai. An inter-island flight conversation with a Mainland couple underscored this "pace of life" factor and its prevalence among Kauai's returning visitors. "We snorkel. But what we really do is sit on the lanai, enjoy the view and drink daiquiris," said Theresa. She and her husband Bob have been going to Kauai for fifteen years. They bought their condominium three years ago and have it managed and rented in their absence to offset the cost. They still work in California and aren't ready to retire.

Kauai is the oldest and most northerly of the Hawaiian Islands. It was the first island Captain Cook visited and it was the last to be incorporated into the then kingdom of Hawaii. The first successful sugar plantation was established here in 1835, and remnants of the plantation-era economy and society are still visible. Despite its sugar history, today Kauai's major industries are tourism and diversified agriculture—papaya, banana, guava, taro and livestock. Because of the tourist ambience, art galleries and local craft shops dot the island leading us to dub Kauai the "Gallery Island." There are seven such galleries in Hanapepe alone, supplied by one or more of Hanapepe's many "gentleman artists". There are as many galleries as restaurants—a dozen or more in the small village of Kapaa.

Kauai retains a predominantly rural face except for resort areas and Poipu, home to many stylish hotels and restaurants. Large sections of the island are mountainous and inaccessible, such as Waimea Canyon and the Napali Coast. The north shore is vulnerable to tsunamis and storms. Fortunately, sparse development has kept loss of life and property to a minimum. The interior, Mount Waialeale especially, is subject to landslides and soil avalanches because of the high rate of precipitation (485" per year average). Again, there is little development in these areas and thus little effect on habitation.

There are no cities, just small towns or villages with populations of three to five thousand people. The plantation way of life is still clearly in evidence on the Westside. The Westside extends from Kalaheo through 'Ele'ele, Hanapepe, Waimea and Kekaha to the Barking Sands Pacific Missle Range Facility and Polihale State Park at the end of the road. Green fields of sugar cane and plantation camps give the area the feel of "old Hawaii." The north and south shores are most heavily influenced by newcomers and visitors, while the Eastside, including Lihue is the island's residential hub. The Lihue area, including Hanamaulu and Puhi, is the island's commercial center, the seat of county and state government, airport and the location of Wilcox Hospital, Kauai Community College, a shopping mall and several large discount retail stores.

This island suffered extensive property damage in 1982 and 1992 from hurricanes Iwa and Iniki. The recovery from Iniki has been slow, with some hotels still not open, and some areas still bear witness to the ravages of nature. Ironically the clean up after these storms removed numerous eyesores like abandoned autos, and led to a new generation of housing.

Hurricanes have not affected tourism or out-migration to a great degree. Visitor numbers are up for Kauai and developers are working on a plan to rebuild on the site of the old Coconut Palms resort (long a favorite among three generations of tourists and site of an Elvis movie) in Kapaa.

The Wailua area boasts several hotels, shopping centers, restaurants and the Wailua River, home to the world famous "Fern Grotto." On the west side of the island is Waimea Canyon—the Grand Canyon of the Pacific—and the longest continuous stretch of beach on the island, "Polihale."

The Kauai County general plan is being updated to the year 2020, when the state has estimated the population will rise to eighty-three thousand or more. Community members involved in the planning have been meeting for over a year and most people seem to like what Kauai is today (rural lifestyle, green hills, beaches), and want to minimize change.

The Executive Office on Aging reports that "there were nearly 8,900 individuals sixty years of age and older residing in Kauai county in 1990. This population represented seventeen percent of the total population of 51,177, including all ethnic minorities.

Housing choices on Kauai include rental apartments, condominiums and single-family homes often built near a medical facility or office complex. Home prices range from forty thousand dollars (for a condominium) to more than three hundred thousand for a single family home. The advertised forty thousand dollar condominium probably needs TLC and is typically leasehold. Condominium properties (usually leasehold) can be found advertised in the $60,000 to $100,000 range. Increases in both sales and prices of homes are modest but the trend is clearly upward. As tourism continues to improve on Kauai, so will the economy. Prices will rise accordingly.[xciv]

Volunteer activities, classes and events are available for active seniors. They include: staffing a senior information center (AARP); writing grants for community development; *hula* lessons; producing a radio or television show; and acting in, directing or attending a play produced by community theater groups. Kauai is also home to many top-ranked golf courses. *Golf Digest* rates four of the championship golf courses on Kauai among the top seven in the state of Hawaii, and Wailua municipal golf course consistently ranks in the top one hundred municipal courses in the country.

PUBLIC TRANSPORTATION

Contact: The Kauai Bus, County of Kauai Transportation Agency, 4396 Rice Street, Suite 104, Lihue 96766, 808-241-6410 Bus Passes may be purchased Monday through Friday, 8:00 a.m. - 4:00 p.m.

There are four types of bus services provided:

> Public: Monday–Friday 5:30 a.m. to 7:00 p.m., Saturday 7:15 a.m. to 3:00 p.m. Detailed information on times

and bus stops is available on printed bus schedules or by calling the Transportation office

Paratransit (door to door) service is available for qualified individuals including:

Senior: 60 years and older and registered with the County Transportation Agency

Americans with Disabilities Act

Kauai will appeal to those seeking a home and retirement site off the beaten track. The pace of life is pastoral and unhurried, and those who dream of having a condominium, house, small farm or ranchette are likely to find rugged and rustic sites around the island.

MOLOKAI: THE FRIENDLY ISLE

The tourist literature accurately depicts Molokai's out-of-the-way lifestyle: "Molokai is still like the Hawaii everyone remembers circa 1955, when life was much more rural, leisurely, friendly and relaxed. Molokai is life in the slow lane."[xcv]

The remoteness and lack of development coupled with more-or-less pristine beaches, waterfalls, and rain forests makes Molokai a one of a kind nature retreat which some retirees will want to call home.[xcvi] Molokai still has no high rises and no stoplights. Natural beauty is abundant on this thirty-eight mile long by eight-mile wide island. It is but a fifteen to twenty-minute airplane ride from Honolulu International Airport to the Hoolehua Airport in the mid-section of Molokai. Also, it's nom de touriste, the "friendly isle," carries a connotation of lingering *aloha* among its inhabitants. Molokai also claims to be the birthplace of the *hula*, with an annual festival featuring men and women, young and old, amateurs and professionals. Locals and tourists alike attend and participate in this event.

With the exception of a few tourist-oriented hotels and lodges, the infrastructure and population are light. In 1990 the population of Molokai was 6,717, with the largest group in Kaunakakai (2,658), followed by Kualapuu (1,661). In 1998 the population still hovered around seven thousand, which included the largest number per capita of residents of Native Hawaiian ancestry.

Medical services and entertainment opportunities are thin but adequate. Both are distinctly local in actual practice. Molokai has a hospital, clinic and two highly regarded dentists, but some medical services must be sought in Honolulu or on the island of Maui, which could be a problem for retirees.

Entertainment options for Molokai residents include jam sessions, beach parties, movies, video rental and hiking, biking, swimming, surfing, snorkeling and music at the hotels (3). Mostly, however, the island is blessedwith anexcess of peace and quiet, even isolation, which many retirees seek.

A significant portion of residents migrate for work and scores commute to Maui and even Oahu (by air) to secure employment.[xcvii] Thus, if your needs include part-time employment income or special medical attention this island is probably not suitable for you.

TRANSPORTATION

Molokai is small enough that a bicycle is a useful and practical means of transportation for children and adults. This is good, because there is no public transportation except services for seniors and disabled. Otherwise, friends and an occasional taxi are the options for non-drivers. Hitchhiking is not unheard of. The Maui Economic Opportunity Council provides bus transportation for seniors on Molokai. For more information call 553-3216.

Expensive vacation homes dot the perimeter of the island mixed with humble bungalows and cabins and occasional condominium complexes of the low-rise variety (three story maximum). Subdivisions are inconspicuous and innocuous here compared with other islands.

Some features of Molokai include:

- Oceanfront and ocean view building sites still available—and many sites are remote and unspoiled.
- Utilities and amenities do not extend to all parts of these more remote and less developed areas.
- Molokai has no dairy, no meat processing plant, and there are no auto dealerships.
- Water catchment systems are common on Molokai, although a third of the island is rain forest preserve.
- Kaluakoi resort (an upscale complex featuring golf, tennis, and scuba and snorkel opportunities on Molokai's west end) has building sites from three to forty acres, priced from $75,000 to over $200,000. There is a lot of wide-open space in this area. There were only six people on Molokai's fabulous Pohapaku beach (running over three continuous miles) when we went to take photos.

On the downside, the rural landscape of Molokai is occasionally blighted by derelict farm equipment and abandoned vehicles.

From 1922 until the 1970s, Maunaloa Town was the center of West Molokai's pineapple industry. Today, Maunaloa Town is being rebuilt as an eco-tourist retreat and local retirement center by landowner Molokai Ranch. The town's main street has been revitalized, with 70-year old buildings refurbished, and new buildings constructed in the old plantation style. It is the home of the island's only movie theatres (three—showing first run movies, $4.00 matinees, $5.50 after six o'clock—seniors $3.50), the Village Grill restaurant, and a Kentucky Fried Chicken outlet.

Molokai Ranch, a development and an eco-tourism business, owns approximately one third of the land on Molokai. In addition to "Deluxe Outdoor Lodging Sites", the Molokai Ranch Lodge recently opened with 22 luxurious guest rooms. Ranch activities include horseback riding, mountain biking, nature walks, ocean adventures, and a ropes challenge course, which even active seniors may want to avoid. The ranch is also a working cattle ranch with more than 60,000 acres.

Kalaupapa National Historical Park, located on the Kalaupapa Peninsula on the north shore of the island, contains the historic Hansen's disease (leprosy) settlements of Kalaupapa and Kalawao. Persons with Hansen's disease were forced to live in this remote place from 1866 until 1969. In Kalawao on the windward side of the peninsula are the churches of Siloama, established in 1866, and Saint Philomena, associated with the work of Father Damien (Joseph De Veuster). The area can be reached by air from O'ahu, Maui and from Ho'ollehua, Moloka'i. It can also be reached by foot or mule from upper Molokai (Contact Moloka'i Mule Rides, Inc., a National Park Service concession. 808-567-6088). Damien Tours, owned and operated by a Kalaupapa resident, offers the commercial tour of Kalaupapa (808-567-6171). There is no vehicular access to the park due to the ocean and steep cliffs.

Molokai represents an opportunity to live far from the madding crowd among persons who are noted for their easy ways and friendly manner. Overall, this is how we found it. Molokai is a favorite retreat for Oahu residents escaping the hustle and bustle and those seeking a "backwater."

However, Molokai is small (less than 7,000 people), and small towns can be slow in welcoming newcomers. Hawaiian Sovereignty is an issue there long simmering, erupting now and then in confrontations. "Rock fever" is not uncommon although we did meet several people who had never been to other islands and were none the worse for it. Local residents take pride in the fact that there are no direct flights from the U.S. Mainland. People from rural circumstances are likely to fare well in this uncluttered, relatively undeveloped environment.

If splendid isolation alongside the bounty and beauty of nature appeals to you, the island of Molokai should be on your list of possible retirement sites.

THE CURIOUS CASE OF LANAI: FROM PINEAPPLES TO PLAYGROUND

The island of Lanai is at one of those commonplace crossroads and the consensus it that the future is predictably uncertain.[xcviii] There is promise as controversial privatization and tourism take on a new face. With a population of about 2900 and at just one hundred and forty square miles Lanai is smaller than Molokai and even less developed. Centrally located in the island chain and said to have been a favorite retreat of King Kamehameha, the island offers spectacular ocean vistas and views of Molokai, Maui and Kahoolawe in the distance. It has been touted as the last refuge for those seeking peace, quiet and solace with gourmet touches. Tourism, it was hoped, would supplant declining pineapple production under the Dole label. But the tourist numbers are not sufficient to sustain the island in spite of two recent destination style resorts and a plan to make of Lanai a retreat for the rich and famous. Plans are afoot to privatize and develop the entire island.[xcix]

Lanai's population is sparse, and amenities are thin. However, the Maui Economic Opportunity Council provides bus transportation for the elderly and disabled on Lanai. For more information call 808/565-6665.

Many roads are unpaved and utilities extend only to the plantation areas, Lanai City, and the two resorts that serve the visitor industry. The island is blessed with numerous stretches of unpopulated beaches. It has no stoplights, no fast food restaurants, eight police officers, and little or no crime to speak of. Lanai Theater Playhouse is a 1930s landmark building presenting first run films, occasional plays and special events.

The Lodge at Koele in the uplands has one hundred and two rooms and is not far from Lanai's only commercial center, Lanai City. The larger Manele Bay Hotel is a traditional beachfront resort. The principal attraction is Manele Bay and the adjacent Hulopoe Beach Park. The beach and park facilities are enjoyed by local residents and visitors alike. David Murdock, chairman of Castle & Cooke, Inc, has purchased C&C (who bought most of the island from Dole) which owns 98 percent of Lanai. The company owns the resorts and a development of luxury vacation homes along the rugged coastline of southeastern Lanai. A brochure touts the development as "still a place for Utopian dreamers seeking refuge from a hectic world. So peaceful and secluded, Lanai feels like it belongs to another time. Now Lanai Co. has created a new opportunity to live in this unique paradise."

One $3 million view lot with a panoramic view of the sea is reserved for Murdock.[c]

Lanai <u>is</u> unique among the islands. Devoted to agriculture for over a century it is about to become a restricted habitat and upscale playground for the affluent, a prospect which could render Lanai the most gentrified and insular of all the island save Niihau, a privately owned preserve for a dwindling number of Native Hawaiians.

Curiously there are homesteading prospects on Lanai. In 1994 Dole Food Co. Inc. leased 100 acres to the state to "keep farming going."[ci] The 55-year lease costs the state $100 a year in rent and includes the condition that plans for an "agricultural park" is complete by 2004. Applicants are required to have some farming experience and start-up money for crops and equipment.

Paperwork includes an environmental assessment and business plans. There have been only two applicants for the programs as of this writing. By some accounts this experiment in "home-steading," which is the only genuine homesteading available to non-Native residents, is a case of tokenism and is not a viable program for immigrant retirees.

Although desirable in its remoteness, physical size and environmental beauty, Lanai is of questionable value as a retirement site. It's probable future as an upscale playground will make it affordable for only a few.[cii] In our estimation Lanai will not sustain a retirement community and it has a less than adequate pool of services and amenities for long-term residency.

Lanai could become the most gentrified or "dualistic" island of all, an entire island devoted to recreation and leisure with only negligible agriculture or productive pursuits.

In its projected gentrified and privatized state it may be renamed the wealthy isle or, after our usage above, the *ludenic* isle, a playground for the rich and famous. Unless it is solace you seek to write a novel, effect a religious conversion, or heal a broken heart, we suggest that Lanai is not a suitable site for retirees nor will it sustain a retirement community for the foreseeable future.

NIIHAU: THE FORBIDDEN ISLE

Known as the Forbidden Isle, Niihau is so inaccessible, so "ghettoized," or privatized, we couldn't go there to determine whether or not retirement is a desirable option. We must conclude, therefore that it is not a suitable retirement site.

We find a curious significance in the inaccessibility of Niihau which renders it not unlike the gentrified areas of Maui and the Kona coast of the Big Island. Custom charter fishing boats circle the forbidden shores as "gawkers" seek a glimpse of "primitive" living.

The island, privately owned by the Robinson family who bought it from King Kamehameha for ten thousand dollars, is "off limits" or *kapu* to travelers and tourists[ciii]. Those with Native Hawaiian blood are quantum qualified to join the 200 or so mostly Native Hawaiian residents who still reside there. In literal terms, Niihau remains more or less undeveloped and untainted by the forces of modernization. As a result, by most accounts, the Native Hawaiians, though dwindling in number, retain the language, customs, and practices and "old Hawaii" as nowhere else in the islands. There being little in the way of productive industry and insufficient production of goods to provide for the local population, foodstuffs and other materials are brought in weekly by boat. The only exports are cattle, sheep and turkey ferried to Kauai for slaughter and processing, and manufactured local craft items produced on a literally "cottage industry" basis.[civ]

Emergency medical services are provided by a helicopter service to Kauai or Oahu. Roads are unpaved; services are few. The fishing, is reputed to be as good as anywhere in the islands.

KAHOOLAWE

For the foreseeable future, while the island is earnestly sought as a possession, even a refuge or a residential village by the Native Hawaiian sovereignty movement, Kahoolawe is neither inhabited nor habitable having been used for decades as a practice bombing and artillery range by the U.S. Navy.

Chapter 4

Your Home in the Islands

Once a preferred island has been selected establishing a residence will be the next important consideration. Deciding whether to rent, buy or build depends on your means and needs. All of these options are available on each island. Retirement communities, catered-living or assisted-living residences are also available throughout Hawaii. Each island has different facilities ranging in cost and level of service. Again be sure to take a good look around and gather as much information as you can before making a permanent decision.

RENTING

A common initial option for retirees coming to Hawaii is renting. Rental housing is widely available on all islands, ranging from four hundred dollars a month upwards to thirty-five hundred-plus. Four hundred dollars buys a partially furnished one-bedroom condominium in Hilo for an independent retiree or two. On the high end, Hawaii Kai Retirement Community on Oahu provides a two-bedroom apartment, including three meals a day, maid service and activity planning, for $4,095.00 per month.

The following is a sample of advertised homes and apartments gathered from local newspapers late in 1999. They serve only as rough indicators of the rental market. However, they may be valuable as a baseline for budgeting and comparison.

On Oahu, *The Honolulu Advertiser* classified included an ad for new, affordable studios for seniors at $565 per month including utilities. Other apartments were priced from $450 to $1200. Rental homes listed for $800 to $3000 per month.

We found of interest a *Pacific Business News* report in June 1999 that rental prices in past years "have seen a drop as much as five to ten percent in areas such as Waikiki."[cv] Broker Shirley Onishi said she has seen rent for a typical two-bedroom, two-bath townhouse in the Waikiki area "drop from $1,325 a month a few years ago to $1,125 a month now." While these differences aren't staggering, they are a good indication of the current rental market.

On the Big Island of Hawaii, two newspapers provide classified advertising. *Hawaii Tribune Herald*, serving East Hawaii, listed homes for rent in the Hilo/Puna area for five to fifteen hundred dollars per month, with the majority of listings between six and seven hundred dollars. Apartments were listed from four to seven hundred, with the median around four hundred dollars. Both partially and fully furnished units were available. *West Hawaii Today* offered homes for rent in the Kailua Kona/Kohala/Waikoloa area for just under $600 to $1,200. A one-bedroom apartment rents for approximately $600 to $1,000 per month.

On Kauai, the offerings aren't as numerous, which reflects Kauai's smaller population. The *Garden Isle News* had few rentals available with homes renting for $1,200 to $3,000 per month and apartments ranging from $565 to $1,000.

Maui News listed Wailuku (central Maui) apartments (one bedroom, one bath) for rent at an average of $700 per month. Lahaina area had apartments for $750 and homes up to $2,500 per month. Up country rentals included a two bedroom cottage for $750 and a 3/2 decks and hot tub for $2,350.[cvi]

On Molokai, Broker Ray Miller offers for rent a 3 bedroom beach home for $1200/mo, an older but nice plantation home in

Kualapuu for $700/mo and another large home in Kaunakakai for $1000/mo.[cvii] Mr. Miller had no rentals to offer on Lanai and we were unable to find any advertised in any papers on Molokai or Maui.

BUYING

Renting may not be everyone's choice. Another option is to purchase. Currently, the housing market on each island is favorable to the retiree seeking a home in Hawaii. Hawaii is now a buyer's market. Prices and number of transactions have sagged since 1990 following an artificial boom in the '80s. Recent years have seen a turnaround. Ruth Chang, an Oahu realtor for twenty years, said that while "the prices of luxury homes are going up, lower to mid-priced homes are still low... now is a good time to buy." [cviii]

In August 1999, Mike Skarlz, chief of research for Prudential Locations, reported that "after eight years of a long, slow descent into night, sun is beginning to shine on the Hawaiian real estate market again. [The] recovery is being driven by the best housing affordability conditions in more than twenty years." Skarlz goes on to note that "thanks to the national economy, the neighbor island markets are enjoying a surge in interest from offshore buyers, particularly those from the West Coast."[cix]

The first time Hawaii buyer may be confused by listings that include FS (fee simple) or LS (leasehold) designations. This refers to whether the land may or may not be purchased outright. Fee simple means that the owner buys the land with the house (or condominium). Leasehold means that the buyer does not buy the land under the house and must pay rent to the landowner.

Water catchment systems may be a new concept to newcomers. Rainwater is collected in a catchment tank for use in the home. Subdivisions without a water system or hookup to the county, as well as homes in the country, are often on catchment. These systems need cleaning and treating much like a swimming pool. As homeowners get older, these maintenance demands may become onerous. Rainwater catchment is found more on the rural islands, especially the island of Hawaii, where almost half of the rurally situated homes on the island have catchment systems.

While the market on each island has special characteristics, overall prices are down and bargains are available. These include both condominium and single family dwellings as well as contracting for construction, rehabilitation of existing housing and owner-builder options. For an overview of residential home prices 1989-1999, see Table 4-1.

Oahu housing trends are provided quarterly by the Honolulu Board of Realtors and First Hawaiian Bank. The results are summarized below. The Oahu housing market expansion, which started in July 1997, has continued into a tenth consecutive quarter. Overall fourth quarter housing resales bested last year's by 11.1 percent, rising to 1,625 units. By housing category, there were 743 single family homes and 882 condominiums reported sold through the Multiple Listing Service system. Comparing these sales figures to past years', Oahu achieved the best fourth quarter (1999) results for single family dwellings and condominium sales since 1989. Condominium resales were the highest for any fourth quarter since 1993.

Median sales prices, after increasing in the third quarter, resumed their slide. The single-family home median price slipped 4.7 percent since last quarter and 3.4% compared to a year ago, to $285,000. The median price paid for a condominium declined to $122,500, a drop of 5.4 percent from last quarter and 5.8 percent for the year.

Economic forecasts for Hawaii have generally turned positive. There are predictions of inflation-adjusted growth of between 2 and 3 percent in Hawaii's ailing economy, which remains behind the Mainland's projected 4 percent growth rate. Tourism figures are up with over 7 million visitors projected for the year 2000 and Hawaii's hotels have witnessed increased occupancy and greater revenue per available room. Choice properties are commanding premiums over and above the list prices. Financing may become an issue, as both long and short-term interest rates have risen a point and a half during 1999. This means fewer families can qualify for loans. In this area, retirees with pensions, marketable securities and savings may have an advantage as buyers.

The following is a sampling of median Oahu housing prices from the fourth quarter of 1999 (Source: Honolulu Board of Realtors quarterly report):

Waikiki:
Condo, $130,000
Kaneohe:
Single family, $295,000
Condo, $137,500
Central Oahu/Mililani:
Single family, $259,500
Condo, $99,500
North Shore:
Single family $244,500
Condo, $104,000
All Oahu:
Single family, $285,000
Condo, $122,000

Average sales prices on Maui as of January 31, 2000 are as follows (Source, Maui Board of Realtors):
Central:
Single family, $311,261

    Condominium, $114,750
Kaanapali:
    Single family, $853,333
    Condominium, $414,600
Kihei:
    Single family, $265,445
    Condominium, $156,375
Lahaina
    Single family, $245,000
    Condominium, $466,500
Makawao:
    Single family, $285,214

There are signs of recovery, but it is likely to be slow and incremental, lasting for perhaps another decade. With the Hawaii senior population projected to increase, this housing market niche is likely to be a strong and active element of recovery.

Starting in the 1970s through the 1980s, demand was made "effective" by large amounts of cash from Japanese buyers and investors. Sale prices went up accordingly.[cx] Since the onset of the 1991 recession, prices have stabilized and even declined notably. This makes for reasonably favorable "buy in" conditions for the retiree. Realtors observe that prices, especially for existing housing, have fallen to mid-1980s prices and, therefore, good values exist throughout the island chain.

Unless you are applying for a mortgage, there is usually no reason to have an appraisal to determine the fair market value of the property. In *Open House, a guide to buying and selling Hawaii real estate*, Roy Kodani says, "Your real estate broker should have enough information, based on past sales, to advise you whether a price is fair or not."[cxi]

Not all factors, certainly not all negative factors, are reflected in the asking price, which presumably is based on comparable sales.

New housing starts have increased as of September/October, 1999, and more are on the drawing boards as the more courageous and resilient developers look ahead to 2010 to 2020.

Restrictions, whether imposed by the county, or by the developer or seller who must be in compliance with land-use laws, determine land use as well as availability. Be sure your property is zoned residential or agricultural land as appropriate. Zoning and land use hassles are not uncommon..

First-time buyers are advised to educate themselves about local laws and building conventions. Also, rely on licensed contractors and inspectors when assessing defects, clouded titles and neighborhood assets and defects.

A downside of tropical living is ants, termites and dry rot. All warrant special attention. Rehabilitation and termite work can cost thousands of dollars and affect sales prices by as much as thirty percent. Ask to see permits, history of sales and occupancy, neighborhood and subdivision master plans, and documentation on title, construction and improvements—especially major overhauls.[cxii] Houses in Honolulu, for example, date back as far as one hundred and fifty years, and some are in dire need of repair. Buyers and sellers should also be aware of "dual agency," a dubious practice that can lead to conflict and legal hassles. Dual agency refers to a broker acting as agent for both the seller and the buyer. Retain a buyer's agent if possible and be prepared to pay part of the commission on the sale.

The housing market in Hawaii especially benefits the retiree who will, after age sixty, owe almost no property taxes, and whose pension is likewise exempt from taxation. In general, retirement dollars, despite the "Paradise tax" and cost of living, will stretch further than any time in the past twenty years in Hawaii. Bargains are available as the market bottoms out on both urbanized Oahu and the rural islands.

While the market is good, it still varies from island to island. On Oahu, for example, land and housing prices are decidedly elevated following the laws of supply and demand. In *The Price of Paradise* it's noted that "land scarcity is a major factor in skyrocketing housing prices. Out of forty major cities Honolulu has the least (amount of) land potentially available for housing." Paradoxically, at the same time land is developed and prices rise, more and more people find Hawaii affordable and desirable. *Pacific Business News* reported in November 1999 that the median asking price of a home on Oahu was $339,900, up 1.5 percent from 1998.

The best bargains, if you can call them that, are in the four hundred to six hundred thousand dollar range. Single-level houses—four to six-bedroom, three to four-baths—that went up fast in the Japanese buy-in of the 70's and 80's are now available at twenty to fifty percent below their previous purchase price. The recession in Asia and uncertain Japanese stock markets have affected the real estate market in Hawaii in the form of foreclosures and bankruptcies.

FEE SIMPLE VS. LEASEHOLD

Hawaii's leasehold practice and lease and conversion laws have been extremely controversial. As much has been written about it, we will only briefly touch the subject as it affects retirees and those considering a move to Hawaii. For detailed treatment(s), see *The Price of Paradise Vol. II*, "Leasehold Conversion," Neal Milner "How should the leasehold controversy be resolved?" and *Land and Power in Hawaii*, Chapters one and three.

The buyer of residential leasehold property including single family dwellings, apartments or condominiums, does not own the land on which his/her home sits and must pay ground rent at various rates and under various conditions. The ground lease is a lease of land only, usually for a long term, such as fifty-five years or more from the original date of the lease.

Fee simple, sometimes called fee simple absolute, is the most complete form of ownership. Fee simple means the buyer purchases the land outright, and acquires ownership of the entire property, including both the land and buildings. The fee simple owner does not pay ground rents, but does pay maintenance fees[cxiii] and real property taxes. Generally speaking, fee simple prices will be higher than leasehold.

Buyers of leasehold property may pay a mortgage and a monthly or annual fee (lease) for the land. Also, leasehold property owners have no control over their monthly housing expense, which is especially burdensome on elders with fixed incomes.

If you are considering a home purchase on leasehold land you should consult a local attorney about your options and obligations.

HIDDEN HOUSING MARKET

The previous discussion has rested on the conventional assumption of sellers meeting buyers in an open market. i.e. the Sunday paper, Open Houses, etc. There is another level of economic activity, part of the underground economy, the hidden market which is usually called the hidden housing market. The Hawaii "hidden housing market" is like an Easter egg hunt: the prizes are hidden in plain sight. All you have to do is go and find it. The "hunt" is part of the fun.

The hidden housing market is not really "hidden" at all, but it does require your presence in the islands. Bargains can be found in various forms, whether they are remote, lack full utilities and amenities, or require completion, refurbishing or remodeling. For some retirees this is a made-to-order, do-it-yourself market that lies beneath the agencies, multiple-listing services, and the real estate section of the Sunday newspaper.

In Hawaii, there is a growing "for sale by owner" movement. Some join an advertising co-op, list on the internet, or just put "For Sale" signs on the front lawn. If you are looking in a particular neighborhood, a regular drive-by will keep you up-to-date in your search. The advantage for both buyer and seller is that the sales price is usually adjusted for closing costs, and sales commission. Additional savings may be found with owner financing, such as elimination of loan fees and appraisal costs. A good rule as always is get it in writing as negotiations take place. Many of these for sale by owner transactions occur in the interstices of family networks, co-workers, or church members. Some sales occur on a less than arm's length basis. As with job search the more people who know you are looking the more likely you are to find a suitable home.

Do not overlook the value of an experienced real estate agent who has access to "hip pocket listings." Tom Ochwat, author of *Hawaii Real Estate Investment Guide,* explains that "these are properties that individual real estate people are aware of that owners are willing to sell and pay commissions on but are not willing to formally sign a contract to list until such time as a realtor brings them a bona fide buyer."[cxiv] (On a personal note, a real estate broker who negotiated a purchase for us later asked if we were interested in selling the same property. Since this was a period of rapid appreciation, and we had fallen out of love with the property, we were indeed interested.)

Banks are also good sources of foreclosed properties. Call an office and ask for their REO (Real Estate Owned) list.

Tax sales are another option and occur on all islands at regular intervals. You must be present to take advantage of them. Information on properties, date of auction, inspection schedule, etc. is available at the office of real estate property tax on each island. Ads are placed in local newspapers about these sales, but most residents don't have the extra money needed to take advantage of these bargains because they are making just enough to support their family.

Some leads are available only through owners or current residents. Such information is often underground or "hidden" even from real estate agents, speculators, and inspectors. Some are available but off the market to certain ethnic groups. A grapevine of local contacts, with or without licensed agents, is the source of such information—only a local presence will find it.

BUILDING

Building your own home in Hawaii is a challenging proposition, especially if you are a newcomer or recent retiree. There are numerous unfinished and untended structures scattered throughout the islands, evidence of poor planning, insufficient capital, or unanticipated events.

Only a few houses in Hawaii have basements or attics, and many frame and rock structures have single-wall construction, suggesting an ease and economy of self-directed construction not widely practiced on the Mainland. Beware of rules and regulations and compliance and permits. Many people use a contractor who has experience wading through the permit process rather than spend the time themselves. Permits are also produced on Hawaiian time[cxv] and can be faster or slower depending on whether you are related to someone at the county. It can take as much as two months (after applying for permits and presenting plans for review) before you can build. Ranges of three to eighteen months to complete construction have been given as estimates.

Despite the problems one is likely to encounter planning, designing and building one's own habitat-residence it is an opportunity for self-expression, building to your personal scale and taste, and (with enough sweat and imagination) economizing with your budget and resources.

Three Options:
1.   Build a cabin or minimum house, and let it evolve according to your means and needs.
2.   Plan and build with an eye to finality and long-term use into your elder years (e.g. single story, handicapped access, etc.)
3.   Buy an existing structure (fixer or unfinished) and expand, modify, or revamp it for your retirement, e.g. game room, exercise room, music room, herbarium, aquarium.

Building your home can also be a component of your retirement process. Most everyone in Hawaii knows someone who has been building his or her "dream house" for six-plus years. There are a few reasons for this. One is that you don't need much to keep you from the elements—a floor, a roof and walls will make a dry home while life and building go forth. Also, owner/builder regulations are lax, allowing much time to pass without completing construction.

If you are serious about building, architects, builders and contractors are available on each island. Talk to several and ask to see examples of their work before choosing. Suppliers of lumber, complete kits, etc., are also doing a brisk business. Some experienced residents advise buying lumber from the Mainland and shipping it here. They say even with the cost of shipping, it is less expensive than prices in the islands.

Many owner-builders have designed their own homes and hired a construction crew to build it. Be aware that the building time in Hawaii, as compared to the Mainland, is relatively longer in spite of the favorable weather. Expect a longer-than-average period for lot preparation securing materials and actual construction.

We advise that if you are not a good carpenter/plumber/painter, you don't attempt extensive remodeling projects. Competent, reliable help is in short supply in Hawaii. Some people have relatives or friends visit them and work for their vacations. Others, with money to burn, import whole construction crews from California.

We took an informal survey of realtors on each island and established a price range to build: between seventy-five to one hundred and fifty dollars per square foot for conventional construction. These prices can be improved by twenty to thirty percent by building a kit home or an octagonal house.

With lot prices from five thousand dollars—you really have to look for these[cxvi]—to twenty-five thousand you can build a kit home for twenty to thirty thousand dollars and have a complete package for under sixty thousand. In an incomplete list of building suppliers/contractors provided as examples, Argus Building Supply in Hilo has kit homes for $7,295 and up. Mr. Argus Johnson, owner, reports that he has sold kits to retirees from Oahu and the west coast. These people are happily going about building their home as a retirement project. Another supplier is Big Island Package Homes—they offer a 2 bedroom, 1 bath, 640 square foot package for $13,250.

Source Tropical (808/254-4002) has built tropical habitats on all islands in Hawaii as well as American Samoa and Guam.[cxvii]

For those interested in home power, a look at *Home Power Magazine* on-line at www.homepower.com will cover questions regarding home power (Guerrilla Solar, water purification, photo voltaic, etc.) Scott Schafer of Molokai Solar provides materials and consulting for solar, hot water, refrigeration, pumps and other materials. *Mother Earth News* Magazine is an excellent source of information on garden and home care and related products. Try out their website: www.motherearthnews.com. Also see Country Living and other rural lifestyle publications.

For contractors and building supplies look for advertisements in the home section of newspapers such as *The Honolulu Advertiser* and local papers on the other islands.

Following the last hurricane on Kauai, insurers require building on pole or stilts for houses that are on the coast. Various designs including concrete blocks, native wood and metal poles are now seen on Kauai's coastline. In coastal areas one will find special codes and building requirements for building "against the weather." E.g. tsunamis and hurricanes. (See especially Kauai County Codes.)

Building on the island of Hawaii may present some difficulties in active or potentially active volcanic areas. In 1983 Kilauea Volcano erupted, destroying about one hundred and twenty homes on the eastern shore of Hawaii. Property is very reasonable in lava flow areas, but because of the risk, few insurance companies will cover homes in these areas. Some people opt for replaceable housing. If the structure blows away or is covered with lava, they just replace it. This has occurred in Kalapana on the Big Island when many homes burned in 1984.

Other possibilities may be found on Hawaii, such as kit homes, prefabricated homes, and homes made of recycled materials. A single woman of our acquaintance had her home built without wood—and not a single tree died.

After much research and time spent living in Hawaii, she decided to build a unique home in a subdivision south of Hilo. This subdivision has county water, electricity and paved roads.

"I'm a single woman, so I can't be worrying about termites, dry rot or fire," she said. The materials to build her house are termite and dry rot-proof. The house is also fireproof, so she doesn't need fire insurance. How about the cost of these materials? Are they higher than conventional building? Glenna assured us they aren't. "Not only is it a comfortable and almost indestructible home, but I saved money," she told us.

Her building materials supplier, who lives in Hilo, is happy to discuss the use of recycled Styrofoam and milk cartons used as building materials. The process is similar to bale houses built from straw bales, then covered with cement. Similarly, we just heard of a concrete block made from hemp. Only in Hawaii!

VIRTUAL HOMESTEADING

While "homesteading" as such is restricted to Native Hawaiians by virtue of 1924 legislation, we shall hit on this topic briefly as it may constitute an emerging pattern of habitation, especially on the rural islands.[cxviii]

There is an increasingly common and easily identifiable pattern of habitation in Hawaii most aptly referred to as "virtual homesteading." It carries vague traces of the American pioneer spirit and recaptures the effort to tame and subsequently close the Wild West. This spirit is alive and well and taking further root on all islands. Proponents use what the environment affords and adding stand-alone or independent infrastructure such as solar water heating, solar and wind power and electric generation. On the Mainland this is a hybrid of the do-it-yourself and the back-to-the-earth movement, which took root in the 60s and 70s in the mid-west, western tier states and Canada. It is also replicated in other island environments, notably the Caribbean, the Bahamas, the South Pacific and the Virgin Islands where the stand-alone habitats are becoming commonplace.

The key elements are an independent spirit and independent (free-standing) technology, including items such as diesel generators, propane refrigerators, chemical toilets, and solar-powered battery systems.

In many rural areas rainwater catchment systems are used instead of drilling a well or hooking up to the county water supply. James Ahsam, a sales rep for Puna Water Services on the Big Island, told us that $5,000 would purchase a complete system including tank, liner, pump, gutters and sterilizer.[cxix]

There are many virtual homesteads in Hawaii on all islands. Some are very creative, at all levels of expense from crude-but-elaborate camps to hi-tech habitats with back-up systems, on-site water and sewage processing, and elaborate electrical power generation.

With the evolved gadgetry of virtual homesteading one can live in the wide open spaces, those that are still available and accessible with something more than a two-wheel drive vehicle and something less than a tank, with a modest outlay in hardware, a minimum of technical know how, a modicum of maintenance, and above all, no monthly utility bills for life. This is no longer survivalist living nor is it less than creature comfort. Thoreau would have approved. So would Emerson, Frank Lloyd Wright, Buckminster Fuller and Lewis Mumford each of whom favored and fostered such approaches to housing and habitation. It meets the minimalist criteria for economy and, when suitably arranged and installed is practical, convenient, and more efficient than many of the alternatives. Above all it has a minimum impact on the environment and does not tax public facilities.

Hawaii, bless its Eden-like climate, is an altogether desirable location for virtual homesteading on a grand scale, although mostly it is the domain of independents, iconoclasts, erstwhile drop-outs, reformed Luddites, and that peculiar breed of Hawaii-philes, the end of the roaders.[cxx] For all that, it is an alternative with endless and very imaginative variations that are played out on back roads and backwaters all across America, but nowhere are the conditions so favorable with ample sun and rain in many areas of the islands.

As the technology has evolved so have the options for free-standing habitation and lifestyle relatively free from the constraints and concerns of urban life. Sustainable habitation based on minimalist lifestyles and the fast developing technology of virtual homesteading is likely to be a part of Hawaii's future as the quest for open space and housing continues. A substantial number of such dwellings using "alternative" technologies and employing virtual homesteading options are already present in the outlying areas and especially the undeveloped areas of the rural islands.

We met a few of these pioneers living, in some cases, not only off the power grid, but off the tax key maps as well – and unknown to the county, the state and the U.S. Census and even the Post Office. Some of these independent minded folk are impecunious freeloading welfare dependents receiving a monthly food stamp allotment and getting health care from "free" clinics. Increasingly, though their numbers include dropouts, burnouts, and those retired from one stressful occupation or another seeking their vision of Paradise without the traffic, congestion, shopping malls, and fast food restaurants most of us take for granted.

Another free-spirit of our acquaintance conceived and constructed a truly unique habitat on the downward slopes of Mauna Kea. Sal-Technically and lawfully this woman lives in a "storage shed or barn," meant to house farm equipment, animals, fertilizer and such. In fact, she lives in an altogether clean, modern and comfortable structure of two rooms with a spectacular ocean view and two walk-in closets (a pantry and a linen closet) approximately 15 x 40 feet. She has no bedroom as such but sleeps in a screened in room on a futon. A casual observer might assume she lives sub-standard. Hardly so. She has refrigeration, hot water on demand, a washer and, au natural, a solar clothes dryer. She has a stereo system, a computer, a cell phone, and a four-wheel drive vehicle. She chose to exclude television from her life although both broadcast and satellite TV are available to her. If she does without any amenities it is hardly a source of complaint or inconvenience but a worthwhile trade-off on items and appliances and conveniences she feels are not needed in the first place. Her tax burden is barely felt as she lawfully resides on a small agricultural plot that is little more than an ordinary vegetable garden.

Beyond habitation, virtual homesteading entails a lifestyle and standard of living not suitable for everyone. But if it is good enough for the Boeing family of Seattle, who maintain a virtually freestanding habitat with private beach and waterfall just beyond Hana, Maui, it is good enough for folks of more modest means who are relocating to the rural areas of Hawaii, Maui, Molokai and Kauai in increasing numbers.

One interesting species of construction and habitation is the several octagons and hexagons which proliferate throughout the islands. They are moderately expensive in kit form but can easily be built on pier and post on even the most jagged and sloping of terrain. They are still one of the least expensive ways to enclose space, recapitulating many round, octagonal, or hexagonal structures such as yurts, teepees and igloos known around the world and throughout history. When placed on a "view" site the result is a commanding and panoramic vista with no visible wires, pipes, or obstructions.

THE BED & BREAKFAST (B & B) PHENOMENON:
Buyer Beware or so you want to be in the Inn business

The phenomenal growth of B&B travel accommodations marks the success of this "cottage industry" approach to inn keeping and an alternative to massive hotels and destination resorts. These more or less one-on-one lodgings provide an alternative that takes the traveler into the homes and communities of the host site and culture. They are now commonplace on the rural islands of Kauai, Maui, and Hawaii. There are now a multitude of such enterprises run by retirees who undertake B&B guests to supplement their incomes and cover part of the costs of relocation and construction. What appears as a natural retirement scenario especially for Hawaii may not always live up to expectations.

This path to secure retirement is not to be undertaken lightly. Marketing, as well as a sound business plan, is essential. Insurance can be problematic and compliance with local regulations and codes a burden. Accommodations must meet minimum standards and are subject to inspection. If your retirement scenario includes a B&B be advised, it takes 2-3 years to build a clientele. If you don't have the means to establish a following, buying into an existing enterprise with an established clientele is preferred. Also, for certain market segments, competition is keen, e.g., eco-tours. The cottage industries of the '90s must count among its practitioners those who have always yearned to be in the Inn business.

Hawaii is awash with bed and breakfasts, ranging from tents and cabins that give you a view of the stars through the roof to elegant rooms graced with family heirlooms, antiques and served with herbal teas, saunas and spas, and stories of old Hawaii. Some retirement plans are successful applications of this approach, but many a retired couple have limped their way back to the

Mainland somewhat wiser and poorer for the experience. For some, of course, a B&B operation is a convenient shelter of assets, and for others it is a cornucopia of deductions for amenities that accrue primarily to the owner-operator. (Saunas and swimming pools top the list, with "horse ranches" and "gardens" not far behind.)

CATERED LIVING

Renting, buying and building are widely available options all over Hawaii. Other retirement options such as nursing homes and assisted living, though they do exist, are few in number, and concentrated in certain areas on Oahu and Maui. Yet with new retirees coming to Hawaii every day, the trend is growing as facilities are being planned, built and expanded. In the meantime, Hawaii does offer a range of retirement residences from catered living to assisted living to complete care nursing homes.

Catered living is a fairly new concept that is growing in popularity. Essentially it is for the retiree who is able-bodied and desires more options, more luxuries, and more amenities. We were first introduced to this idea about fifteen years ago in Oakland, California, when helping an older friend relocate and settle in the Bay Area. We were able to find a "senior hotel," offering room, maid service and two or three meals a day for eight hundred dollars a month. We were ready to move in, except for one detail—at that time we were a few years shy of age fifty-five!

The Ponds at Punalu'u, on Oahu, is a catered living facility. They offer the following package of services and amenities: three meals per day served restaurant style in the Waimea Dining Room, all utilities except phone and cable television, regular housekeeping services, washers and dryers on each floor, social, educational and cultural programs and outings, scheduled transportation to physician appointments, and a twenty-four-hour emergency call system. Among the other offerings are a skilled nursing facility and a "scaled" nursing care and Alzheimer's care unit. This is made to order for couples where one or the other suffers from a chronic condition and requires periodic hospitalization. Monthly rates are $1,095 to $3,895 for an efficiency to two-bedroom suite. For a second person add $595. The Ponds has no entrance fee.

Catered living at the Ponds at Punalu'u was specifically designed for healthy seniors seeking to escape the mundane responsibilities of independent living, the better to enjoy their golden years. The mission at the Ponds is to "release retirees from the tedious tasks of house cleaning, grocery shopping, cooking, yard work, etc."[cxxi]

Retirement residences are similar to catered living, and may be the answer for seniors who are tired of the responsibility of home ownership but still enjoy an active lifestyle. Craig Matsunaga with Holiday Retirement Corporation reports that eighty percent of the population at Hawaii Kai (a retirement residence on Oahu) is seventy-five to eighty-five-years old and very active. Several of the residents have a daily routine consisting of breakfast followed by golf the rest of the day at a course two miles away. Some go shopping, swimming or play bridge in town. The management is always looking for new activities and attempts to cater to the needs of their client/residents. Residents are enthusiastic about the living arrangement. One woman commented, "I miss cleaning my own house like I miss a headache."

Assisted living is less-than-complete care as found in a nursing home. A helpful website for elderly information, www.Healthgrades.com, defines it as "a congregate residential setting. What sets an assisted living residence apart from a nursing home is that assisted living does not provide continuous skilled nursing care." This type of facility targets those who need assistance with two or more daily activities such as bathing, dressing, eating and taking medications. *Pacific Business News* reported in November, 1999 the proposed construction of an assisted living site in West Oahu, the first of its kind there. Additional services will be three meals a day, weekly linen service and van transportation. See Table 4-2 for more information.

On Maui there are several options for seniors needing help, ranging from complete care to home care. And now Hale Makua, Maui's largest provider of nursing homes and home health care for seniors, expects to buy a 4.8-acre site in the Kulamalu subdivision and provide up to eighty units of elderly housing for people who need personal care. The sixty-plus group in the Kula-Makawao region of Maui is its primary potential market. The monthly fees are expected to run twenty-five hundred to thirty-five hundred dollars with a projected opening by the end of 2001.

Another fairly recent idea in retirement living is a retirement community. A retirement community attempts to combine all the needs and wants of seniors in a "community-type" setting. This approach to retirement evolved some years ago in southern California and Florida. The influx of the over-fifty-five retiree group sought housing and extras, such as on-call medical services, transportation and recreation activities to fill a widening gap between complete self-sufficiency and total dependence. The result is a sophisticated and comprehensive approach to retirement living at any age with everything from wake-up calls to on-site ambulances available at a moments notice.

On Oahu, Phase I of Hawaii Kai Retirement Community, with one hundred and ninety-three rooms, was ninety-six percent full at the end of its first year. Monthly rents (this is month to month arrangement with no lease or buy-in cost) at Hawaii Kai range from $1,895 to $2,140 a month for studios, to $4,095 to $5,095 for two-and-three-bedroom garden cottages. Phase II will add an additional one hundred and seventy-five units. Another project, Kalama Heights Retirement Residence in Kihei, Maui, is scheduled for completion in 2000. Monthly rents will range from $1,700 to $3,500. The Hawaii Kai Phase II and the Kihei projects will each have swimming pools.

Maui Lani Retirement Community, in planning stages for some time, will eventually consist of 15.5 acres containing ninety independent living, ninety assisted-living and forty skilled nursing units. The planned senior community is to be built near the Maui Memorial Medical Center.[cxxii] These residence communities also provide assisted-living at additional cost.

At the Arcadia Retirement Residence in Honolulu, entrance fees are rather high at $89,200 to $257,300, but cover lifetime residency. An additional service charge provides for all meals, a weekly maid service, linen service, maintenance, utilities, security and general health care protection. These monthly charges are $1,324 to $2,637. Arcadia has a capacity of two hundred and fifty units and sixty skilled-nursing facility beds. The Arcadia also provides assisted living, skilled nursing and special care at additional cost for those who develop Alzheimer's or dementia. In order to become a resident of Arcadia you must be at least sixty-two years old.

Regency at Hualalai, is a 129-apartment community. This project will be the first state licensed assisted living retirement facility for the Big Island of Hawaii. The apartments are located on 5.2 acres near Kailua-Kona. Floor plans offer studio, one and two-bedroom units. Services included in the cost of monthly rent are: up to three meals per day, weekly maid service, transportation, and valet parking. A selection of amenities is as follows: dining rooms with restaurant-style service, pool and spa, library, wellness programs, vacation exchange program with sister communities in Washington and Oregon.

As it is now, prices for these residential units may be out of reach for the middle-income or fixed-income retiree. Scaled down, less expensive facilities are available, but they are few in number and vary widely in quality of service and level of care.

Senior apartments and homes, ranging from luxury to low-income, are available near community senior centers and/or hospitals and medical centers. More information may be obtained from the Office on Aging on each island. (See Table 4-3, which includes telephone numbers for Offices on Aging by island.)

Those who wish an interim situation between ordinary hotels and buying, leasing or building a house, would do well to sample such senior residential living arrangements, especially seniors who do not wish to live alone. Such facilities are very likely to proliferate in the coming decades on each of the islands as the population ages and as demand rises. Most facilities welcome "prospects" and will be happy to give you a free tour which often includes lunch.

PRESERVING THE VILLAGE WAY OF LIFE

If you seek a slice of Hawaii's rural lifestyle, as many have and many more will, be aware of the problematic nature of maintaining and preserving the rural ambience and the village mode of residential development that once characterized both the "outer" islands and practically all of Oahu.

Preservation of rural towns, villages and "countrified" subdivisions are the best hope and worst fear for Hawaii's future. They are a way to anticipate growth and can generate a system of regulated development and a fair and orderly process of meeting the needs of the populace. Alternatively, if poorly drafted and legislated in a partisan manner, the subdivision planning process can lead to disproportionate and inequitable tax burdens, endless repetition of look alike tracts and ever higher costs. This can foster undue stratification and lead to ghetto like conditions before they are completed. Witness the "miracle" of high-rise construction of the 1950s and 1960s a solution to urban sprawl that backfired in nearly every major American city.[cxxiii] It comes down to a choice between a planned environment, and a planned and budgeted future, versus unchecked random development driven by the profit motive alone.

In *The Price of Paradise*, local architect and planner Francis Oda[cxxiv] proffers a vision of villages as self-sufficient or "sustainable communities." He believes that the residents of Hawaii can base a new vision on the premise that housing, agriculture and tourism are not only compatible but essential to each other's viability.

> Close your eyes again and picture this; modern housing clustered like the old plantation villages and surrounded by tree farms of bioengineered native hardwoods, macadamia orchards, dry land taro lands, seed corn plots, botanical gardens, community gardens, individual garden plots, and banana patches. Imagine these villages focused around little centers with a convenience store, churches, postal service, day care center, and even a McDonalds...[cxxv]

This aptly describes many a rural village and plantation town still visible today on each of the islands. Can they be sustained? Will they give way to strip malls and stoplights as they have to Laundromats, ATM's, and fast food franchises that today accompany even the smallest hamlet? Does development inevitably produce urbanization, even when we dub it ruralization? Will it spoil the rural islands as it has Oahu, which let it be said, was not so very long ago as "rural" as Maui and Kauai?

Despite the vistas and seemingly "vast" open spaces of the Big Isle[cxxvi] the Kona and North Kohala areas show preliminary signs of over-development with ocean view lots in the millions of dollars. The Kona Master Plan seeks to avoid continuous shoreline development and retain "green" and "open" spaces. All parties to planning in the islands seem to favor maintaining open spaces, view corridors, green or pastoral areas, parks, and accessible beaches. Several remedies have been proposed. None are completely effective.

On the Big Island, The Puna Community Development Plan (1992) echoes the desires of Kona residents and expresses some of the same concerns regarding crowding, infrastructure, and development as those heard in the concrete bowels of Waikiki. Puna is a large district in East Hawaii with a population composed of working class families and middle class retirees. Residents there wish to maintain the village and rural feeling of the area, but also seek schools, parks, improved roads and upgraded public services.

To develop or preserve? This dilemma is a two-edged sword driving and complicating land use on all islands. While most notable on Oahu, the process is making itself felt on the rural islands as well, especially North Kona and South Maui. [cxxxvii]

In the expansive Puna and Kau areas large subdivisions developed in the 1960s and 1970s led to controversy over "off grid" and "non-conforming" subdivisions with insufficient or nonexistent water, fire and emergency services. The subdivisions were not always well planned and were a breeding ground for substandard and, in some cases, blighted housing. It is home, first or second, permanent or vacation, to hundreds of retirees, with eighty thousand lots and parcels available at truly modest prices ($4,000 to $40,000 per acre). There is room for growth, but infrastructure, schools, parks, open spaces, funding and long-term impact are issues now open to debate.

Preserving the rural lifestyle while seeking subdivision and "citified" amenities is a balancing act facing current and future residents of all the islands. Social activist and regional planner Bonnie Goodell of Puna, Big Island, has proposed what could pass as a model to other islands, namely, a new land use designation, the Rural Town District (RTD). Such a designation would limit development and allow small, local village entities to retain their identity as "country" or "pastoral" or "rural" by adopting the RTD designation for local control of development.

The new category is the result of a community-based planning process. "The most often expressed fear of development was of the traffic-congested lifestyle associated with the current suburban-sprawl pattern."[cxxviii] The RTD code would encourage the preservation of traditional-style rural towns, or the development of new towns in the traditional style, except that they would emerge as individually formed special districts, e.g. the Downtown Hilo District. The RTD code would be available for communities of 2000 or more to use, subject to community initiation and compliance with county master plan objectives.

The village theme sells well but is occasionally subject to ludicrous interpretations and campaigns to convince the traveler-buyer that he or she is truly a participant in "village life" in a village environment rather than a consumer at a destination resort.[cxxix] It is the image that counts so long as it leads to demand for what the image conveys, i.e. a ready buyer.

This can be a problem for well-intentioned retirees. Wanting to be involved or integrated, they nonetheless insulate themselves in their own "world," thereby confirming the perceptions of long term residents that newcomers have no genuine or enduring interest in the activities of the community or "village" at large.

A gated community, now becoming common, does not a village make. Rather it creates an insular ghetto of wealth and privilege, a feature of the emerging Hawaii of the 21st century that should not be overlooked. The leisure class is already present in Hawaii, if not entirely accounted for.[cxxx]

Similarly, each island has spawned its own ghettos of poverty and pockets of welfare as well, sometimes in proximity to the upscale areas, creating a curious mutual "blight" at both ends of the economic scale, one literally within sight of the other.

Residents will disagree as to detail but there is a widespread sentiment to preserve the essential elements (open space, security, infrastructure) of the village way of life, even to absurd lengths, as in Hilton Hawaiian Village, now an icon of Waikiki and the Hawaiian "scene." These commercial establishments are a far cry from such rural motifs found in Hana, Maui, Hanalei Valley, Kauai, or Pahoa or Hawi on the Big Island.

Can this village ambience be preserved and sustained? It's an open and controversial question. Diverse and sometimes conflicting proposals have been put forth by grass-roots groups and international development groups, but the system appears to grind along on both Oahu and the rural islands, creating a checkerboard of land use amid a sea of politics as usual.[cxxxi]

Chapter 5

Health and Healthy Living

For two years in a row Hawaii has been named by independent research groups as the "healthiest" state in the nation.[cxxxii] Hawaii residents have an average life expectancy of seventy-nine years, while on the Mainland the average is seventy-five years.[cxxxiii] Hawaii has led the national average life expectancy for about twenty years.[cxxxiv] A combination of natural environmental factors, lifestyles and genetics accounts for Hawaii's unique status in longevity.

Hawaii's playground is the Pacific Ocean, and the temperate climate permits year-round outdoor activities. However, very specific health hazards also come with the territory.

Overexposure to sun, especially with seniors, may result in life-threatening diseases. Daily television news programs report on the "UV" (ultraviolet) rays that can be intense and cause skin problems, including cancer. Caucasians are especially sensitive, as are fair-skinned Asians. Seniors are forewarned for good reason—overexposure, especially to mid-day sun, can cause sunstroke and worse. Most people experience a really bad burn before they develop respect for Hawaii's sun. It is easy to burn in a short time (one to two hours if you are from a northern clime); those in the know wear sunscreen, hats, and long sleeves and pants when out in the sun for any length of time. Even if you are just on a short ride in an open convertible, beware the cumulative effects of the sun. Sunscreen and insect repellent are essential for any outing.

Another common problem in Hawaii is respiratory ailments, such as asthma and allergies. Flowers and pollen run rampant throughout the "Aloha State." Something is always blooming somewhere in Hawaii, which can irritate sufferers year-round, rather than just in spring. The rain that brings the flowers also brings mold, another serious problem for many people with asthma.

Vog, volcanic fog or volcanic haze, occurs as a result of the ongoing volcanic activity of Kilauea Volcano on the Big Island. Emissions from the volcano contaminate the air with sulfur dioxide, sulfuric acid, sulfates, and various other particles. For some this irritates the lungs and may cause symptoms such as coughing, wheezing and shortness of breath. This affects mainly the Kona Coast and should be a consideration when selecting a residential area.

Leptospirosis is a bacterial infection that can be especially serious in seniors. It occurs after swimming or wading in contaminated freshwater rivers, streams, and ponds or after contact with contaminated moist soil or plants. Infection may also occur after drinking contaminated water. People with catchment systems must take precautions against this. The symptoms, which resemble the flu and occur 2 to 20 days after exposure, include fever, chills, headache, muscle aches, eye irritation, nausea, and vomiting. Antibiotic treatment may be effective if given at an early stage. Other skin conditions resulting from heat or fungus are common as well.

Centipedes, one of the scarier critters around here, sting in self-defense, using the tips of their enlarged first pair of legs, which carry poison glands. Centipede stings can cause intense pain followed by swelling and redness around the wound. These symptoms last for several hours or days. Occasionally, the wound may become infected. Although they are common in Hawaii, centipedes won't kill you. Like bees, spiders and scorpions, they are just a very painful nuisance. Obviously it is best to avoid them. Be especially careful in rental units that have remained unused for a time, as they often lurk there. Eliminate centipedes' food sources, such as cockroaches and slugs. Cockroaches, aside from being unsightly, can be a problem for asthmatics. (Their body pieces and droppings can produce allergic reactions.) Roach, ant and pest traps are readily available in drug and hardware stores.

For the most part, shark attacks provoke scary media coverage. However, they are so rare that they represent a minute fraction of the accidents and fatalities that occur in the state. More people die from drowning than from shark attacks.

Jellyfish attacks in bays and harbors, while uncommon, can be fatal, and swimmers of any age should be cautioned to check infested beaches and waters.[cxxxv] Portuguese Man-of-War stings are not uncommon in Hawaii. They float on the surface of the water with their long, stinging tentacles trailing in the water below. Stings can cause blisters, burning pain and redness. Rinse with salt or freshwater. Persistent itchy rashes can be treated with antihistamines or hydrocortisone cream. Coral scrapes can also be a nuisance.

Senior Services

Services for seniors can be found in some form on all the islands. Certain areas of Hawaii will have more to offer than others. Take, for instance, the facilities on Oahu. Senior residential and elder care facilities offer top-of-the-line services, and nutrition sites are distributed across the island.[cxxxvi] There are multipurpose senior centers available around the island as well. Adult day-care services are available in the districts of Waianae, Wahiawa, Koolaupoko, Ewa and Honolulu.

Oahu boasts the best-developed network of senior services and activities available to retirees and elders, including the disabled. These services include meals on wheels, respite, chore service and senior companion services. Such centers are a good place to start "networking" and procuring information.

On the <u>Big Island of Hawaii</u>, senior nutrition programs are found in the North Kohala, South Kohala, Hamakua, North Hilo, South Hilo, Puna, Ka'u, and South Kona communities. Multi-purpose senior centers are located in these areas, too. Adult day-care services are available in South Kona and South Hilo. The Big Island has seven hospitals, including Hilo Medical Center, North Hawaii Community Hospital and Kau Hospital. On the Big Island, North Hawaii Community Hospital (NHCH) offers leading-edge medical technology beside holistic medicine. Patients can opt for complementary services such naturopathy, chiropractic, acupuncture, massage (shiatsu, lomi, reflexology), psychotherapy and aromatherapy. NHCH was the first hospital in the country to combine high tech and "high touch." Hotels and resorts on the Big Island are featuring yoga, tai chi and meditation along with body wraps and classes in stress management and behavioral and spiritual awareness.[cxxxvii]

Kaiser Permanente has clinics in Kona, Hilo and Waimea with internists, family specialists, pediatricians and pharmacies. Other Kaiser physicians and specialists, such as ophthalmologists and podiatrists, make a circuit from Honolulu and visit the rural islands, usually once a month. Surgery and some tests are done exclusively in Honolulu. Bay Clinic also offers clinics in Hilo, Ka'u and Kona. Private medical care in all specialties is also available through major health plans.

Kauai offers nutrition programs in Waimea, Koloa, Lihue, Kawaihau and Hanalei. Focal points (senior centers or community centers used by senior services) are found in Kawaihau, Lihue, and Koloa. Adult day-care services are available in Lihue. Lihue is home to Wilcox Memorial Hospital, and West Kauai is served by the West Kauai Medical Center. Mahelona Medical Center in Kapaa on Kauai's east side is a hospital and walk-in clinic. For current phone numbers and addresses contact Office on Aging. See Table 4-3.

Maui Memorial Medical Center, located in Wailuku, received a three-year accreditation from the Joint Commission on Accreditation of Healthcare Organizations in 1999 as recognition of a high standard of care. However, the same day that the announcement was made, a complaint surfaced that the hospital was—once again— overflowing with patients who were being held in the emergency room until permanent beds could be found. The hospital is anticipating a thirty-eight million dollar renovation. Valerie Monson reported in a *Maui News* article about the accreditation, May 3, 1999, that "Maui Memorial's resources—as well as those on Oahu—are typically strained during the winter months, especially from January through March, when tourists are at a peak and when winter illnesses affect more residents, especially senior citizens."[cxxxviii]

Hale Makua provides 432 long-term care beds at its Kahului and Wailuku facilities. Maui also has a hospital in Kula which has no emergency services but provides long-term care (99 beds). Ohana Physicians Clinic, located on the Kula Hospital Campus, is a family practice and urgent care facility. Other clinics including Kaiser Permanente are the found in Kihei, Lahaina and Wailuku.

Maui is short on senior care, lacking adult residential care homes (500 homes on Oahu and 60 in Hilo, but Maui has only 13) and enough long-term care beds.[cxxxix]

On <u>Molokai</u>, medical services are thin but adequate. Molokai has a hospital, clinic and two highly regarded dentists, but some medical services must be sought in Honolulu or on the island of Maui, which could be a problem for retirees. The same goes for Lanai, which has even fewer medical facilities to benefit seniors. (See Table 5-1 for a list of Hawaii hospitals. See also Pacific Business News Book of Lists.)

Retirees usually require prescription drugs. These are available at the aforementioned hospitals and clinics, as well as pharmacies. Popular drug stores in Hawaii are Longs and Safeway, which are available on most islands. Wal-Mart also has a pharmacy in some stores.

Just as on the Mainland, Hawaii is served by the 911 emergency medical response system. Hawaii also uses the Coast Guard's search and rescue center and military services to augment the medical response system. Medical flights are also available to rush patients to state-of-the-art facilities in Honolulu. These services are available in all areas; however, response time in rural areas may be longer as parts of Hawaii are underserved. This has been noted, and progress is beginning to fix this essential need.

Special flight considerations are made for seniors and retirees with family on the Mainland. Private services such as Medical Air Service Association (MASA), located in Dallas, Texas, provide urgent transportation for the terminally ill and their families. We have utilized this service ourselves when a parent was ill. Airfare was reimbursed by MASA. Restrictions apply; for more information call MASA at 1-800-643-9023.

HMO and Health Plans

In a recent business news study Kaiser Hawaii ranked in the top twenty HMOs.[cxl] Blue Cross-Blue Shield is also available in Hawaii through Hawaii Medical Services Association (HMSA). However, it is a separate region and thus your existing membership will not transfer from the Mainland. You must enroll in the Hawaii plan. If you are employed for more than 19 hours a week, your employer is required to offer health insurance at his or her expense. Employers usually cover the employee, but not a spouse or children. Employees usually end up paying for additional coverage. Kaiser-Permanente and other plans (such as Kapiolani, etc.) provide for Medicare coverage for those over sixty-five. We suggest, again, that you shop around for the best coverage and prices. Table 5-2 lists different health plans in Hawaii and their addresses.

To die in Hawaii: Hospice

If Hawaii is a permanent retirement choice for you, as it is for us, death on the islands may be inevitable. While it is not a happy subject, you should take it into consideration when making your retirement decision.

Hawaii is as ideal a site as one is likely to find anywhere for a terminal illness, assisted suicide, or even euthanasia. More people come to Hawaii to die than is suspected. As wonderful as Hawaii can be for renewal, for rehabilitation and for recovery, it can be a pacific—literally peaceful—place to die. The significance of this fact will not be lost on future generations of residents.

Governor Cayetano's Blue Ribbon Panel on Living and Dying with Dignity published a final report in May. 1998. After a year spent gathering testimony regarding this issue, the panel concluded that many people unnecessarily face lingering, painful and undignified deaths. What the panel learned during this period of inquiry led to the following unanimous recommendations:

1. That spiritual counseling be made more available to individuals who are afflicted with life threatening illnesses by integrating those services more fully into the healthcare system.
2. That public and healthcare professional education programs be designed and implemented to increase awareness of the choices available to the dying.
3. That the content of Advance Directives for Healthcare, including living wills, be made more specific, their use more widespread and their provisions more binding.
4. That hospice care be made more available and offered more expediently to the dying.
5. That effective pain management and other symptom control programs be required in all licensed healthcare institutions
6. That involuntary euthanasia should continue to be a crime.

Beyond those unanimous recommendations, they considered the alternatives of physician-assisted suicide (PAS) or physician-assisted death (PAD) as a choice for those who hold that it is moral and ethical and who might require the help of their physician to implement that choice. These two options would be available only to mentally alert patients who are either terminally ill or suffer intractable illness that cannot be cured or successfully palliated. As of this writing, no law has been put in place to legalize either PAS or PAD.[cxli]

While there is no "death movement" as such, Hawaii has adopted death with dignity laws. In 1999 the Hawaii Legislature passed House Bill 172 to carry out recommendations of the

Governor's Blue Ribbon Panel on Living and Dying with Dignity. These will require insurers to cover hospice consultations and to pay for bed and board in hospice care homes.

Hospice programs, like those elsewhere, provide support and care for terminally ill persons and their families in the last stages of disease. These services, which include pain relief, symptom management, and supportive services, are provided in the home with arrangements for in-patient care when needed. (See Table 5-3 for a list of hospices in Hawaii.)

The Hawaii Uniform Health Care Decisions Act, effective July 1, 1999, provides a lawful form that allows you to express in writing your wishes for future health care. The form is called an "Advance Directive."[cxlii] One can appoint a health care agent to act on their behalf. One can say what decisions the agent may make, or may provide instructions for a supervising health care provider to follow.

You may designate yourself as an organ donor, and state your health care provider(s). Decisions may also made regarding orders on resuscitation, and directions to provide, withhold, or withdraw artificial nutrition and hydration. The form is only valid if signed voluntarily and if signatory is of sound mind. Forms are available from the Executive Office on Aging,[cxliii] or by calling 808/586-0100.

The University of Hawaii Elder Law Clinic on Oahu and in Hilo are excellent information sources about Advance Directives. Talk with your family before someone is seriously ill. Make sure your friends and/or family members know your wishes just in case you can't speak for yourself, or they are half an ocean away and unable to travel to care for you.

The Executive Office on Aging sponsors the Kokua Mau (kokua—help, assist, support; mau—always, constant, Kokua Mau—continuing help or assistance[cxliv]) project which promotes the right to die in the place of one's choice, relatively free of pain, in maximum possible comfort, and with community support appropriate to one's beliefs and values. For more information contact Kokua Mau at 808/585-977 or info@kokua-mau.org.

Major insurers who cover hospice now cover hospice room and board (as of January 2000).[cxlv] Prior to 2000, covered hospice care was only for in-home services.

Most people do not consciously choose the place, and certainly not the time and circumstances, of their death. However, a substantial number do know that death is approaching, or expected, due to some life-consuming disease or ailment. Those threatened by illness do have choices. A few will deliberately choose Hawaii as a desirable place to die.

Once again the Paradise theme is not too far removed to allow one to conceive moving to a part of the world that surrounds one with natural beauty as death approaches.

While Hawaii is without doubt a beautiful place to die, it lacks enough facilities for assisted living, nursing facilities, and hospice care. Nonetheless, the idea of Hawaii as a hospice center especially on the rural islands is taking hold and finding widespread acceptance. As more and more seniors and elders populate the state the requisite services likely will follow.

Chapter 6

Recreation and Leisure Pursuits

Hawaii offers a wide variety of activities for seniors, ranging from scuba diving to community volunteer work. Hawaii has movie theaters, beaches and restaurants featuring cuisine from around the world. Where you decide to live will affect the range of activities, but each island and community has something unique and exciting to offer.

BEACHES

Hawaii is world renowned for its beaches, beach parks, and playgrounds. Part of the fun of living in Hawaii is the hunt for just the right beach for…swimming, wading, snorkeling, surfing, sun bathing or what have you. There are scores of beaches that will take months or even years to visit so you are not likely to become bored.

We have talked to any number of people who come here because of the outdoor activities, especially the beaches and parks, which are extremely well maintained. Each island has its special beaches with sands of varying colors—black, gold, white, pink and even green (on the Hawaii Island—a green beach is a remarkable sight).

Below we offer our personal favorites—our top ten picks for your perusal. So, pack your sunscreen, your beach bag, and your picnic basket and enjoy the principal attractions of Hawaii one at a time.

TOP TEN BEACHES

I   ALA MOANA BEACH PARK, OAHU This Park is second in popularity and population only to Waikiki Beach. Swimming is suitable for all age groups and facilities (showers, toilets, etc.) are ample except for holiday weekends. Easily accessible by bus or auto it is located adjacent to the equally popular Ala Moana Shopping Center where bathers combine shopping, dining and sun worship.

II   KAILUA BEACH PARK, OAHU This popular family beach park is located on the Windward Shore of Kailua and runs contiguous with Lanikai Beach. It is ideal for swimming, wind surfing, snorkeling; facilities are adequate with a lunch stand, music pavilion and small boat launch. The beach has a slow safe fall with a reef and small islands a short swim away.

III   WAIMANALO BEACH PARK, OAHU This large beach runs over two miles along the eastern windward tip of Oahu and is part of the Waimanalo Bay State Recreation area. Snack stands and lunch wagons frequent the area; showers and toilets are clean and well maintained. The beach is ideal for sunning and snorkeling and is popular with campers and picnickers.

IV   SPENCER BEACH PARK, BIG ISLAND. Spencer Park is popular with Big Island families who come for the day, weekend or longer. The park is also home to camping groups and conferences with ancient ruins and heiaus (sacred Hawaiian shrines) nearby. The water is ideal for swimming, snorkeling and wading. Restrooms, showers, picnic facilities as well as camping areas are some of the amenities of this beach. It is a lovely setting for the special occasion or family gathering. We chose Spencer Beach Park for our wedding. Kawaihae, with a sailboat mooring area, boat launch and three restaurants is a short drive away.

V LYDGATE PARK, KAUAI. Located near the Wailua River, Lydgate Park is one of the most popular parks on Kauai. Two large lava pools, one perfect for kids and the other protecting swimmers and snorkelers, make it a great place to spend the day. Swimming is very good. There are showers, restrooms, and lifeguards. Restaurants and facilities are available nearby.

VI PAPOHAKU BEACH PARK, MOLOKAI This isolated beach offers the best snorkeling on Molokai, perhaps the best in the islands, perhaps the best in the world. Usually uncrowded, on the day we visited, there were six souls on a three mile long beach.

VIII AKENA (OR ONELOA) BEACH, MAUI. Once a hideaway for hippies, the beach today is increasingly popular with mainstream tourists. Considered by some the most beautiful beach on Maui, it may be taken over by mondo-condo development. It was still a hideaway when we visited most recently. Facilities and amenities are lacking at this beautiful South Wailea location.

VIII KEKAHA BEACH, KAUAI Although it is close to the highway, the lovely stretch of white sand beach offers some marvelous picnic spots, but the rough surf and powerful currents make swimming dangerous. Located on the leeward coast of Kauai, Kekaha Beach Park is a 20-acre playground with a view of the island of Niihau, picnic facilities and restrooms. Swimming is good when surf is down.

iX   PUNALUU BLACK SAND BEACH, BIG ISLAND OF HAWAII. Known for its unique sparkling black sand and sea turtles which frequent the shoals Punaluu lives up to its reputation for gorgeous scenery and natural beauty. Facilities and parking are adequate and the area (located eight miles north of Naalehu on the southeast aspect of the Big Island) is rarely crowded.

X   Last, but not least is the venerable WAIKIKI BEACH, and adjacent Duke Kahanamoku Beach Park (at the west end) and Kapiolani Park (at the east end). There you will find mountains of burnt flesh, bikini clad maidens, iron pumping gents and assorted gawkers. Though tarnished by time and refurbished with imported sand it retains its image as THE tourist attraction for all of Hawaii.

HONORABLE MENTION

Although not strictly legal there are many nude beaches located throughout Hawaii. Be sure to apply extra sunscreen to areas not often exposed to nature's elements. Other beaches are frequented and sometimes inundated with motorcycle enthusiasts, fishing advocates, impromptu music groups or religious organizations.

There are numerous small beach parks on Oahu's North Shore running from Waiahole to Waialua. Some of these are "surf" beaches, especially Sunset Beach where surfers brave the world famous "Pipeline." Others are small and cozy with limited parking and a few picnic benches. Still others are decidedly family oriented. No one of these stands clearly above the others; all are fun to explore; most will be populated by local residents on weekends and holidays. If you are the friendly type you may be asked to join in, grab a plate or sing along.

Finally, our personal favorite beach on Oahu is a small almost obscure spot on East Oahu – Makapu'u Beach Park – where Burt Lancaster romanced Deborah Kerr in *From Here to Eternity*.[cxlvi] Legend has it that there discarded street clothes may be found in a rumpled pile in the rocks at the north end of the beach. Across the road is Sea Life Park now a popular tourist site with extensive facilities and aquatic entertainment.

MORE OUTDOOR FUN

People are drawn to Hawaii because of the climate—one can "play" outdoors year-round. Swimming, surfing and snorkeling are some of the more prominent activities that draw active residents to the islands.

Canoe and sailing clubs are popular with all ages; many retired and senior members participate. Selected events from the Hawaii Visitors and Convention Bureau include the following ocean-related activities: outrigger canoe race (Keehi Lagoon next to Honolulu Airport); Hawaiian International Ocean Challenge (Oahu) where teams of international lifeguards compete in eight events; and the ever-popular "Dragon Boat Races." Surfing is, of course, a major activity enjoyed by all ages.

Hiking, running, and biking are among other activities enjoyed by seniors. Many fund-raising programs involve tournaments (golf, tennis) and races/walks. The Honolulu Marathon and the Ironman Triathlon on the Big Island are popular international events.

These are just a few of the activities and recreational opportunities available. The State Parks and Recreation Department offers classes, clubs and activities at centers on each island.

Garden groups, outdoor circles, chapters of the Sierra Club and specialty groups (bonsai, orchids, roses, etc.) meet regularly, have shows and sales often open to the public. Three new books will be of interest to gardeners, new and old. See recommended reading for "A Native Hawaiian Garden," "Growing Vegetables in Hawaii," and "Ethnic Culinary Herbs." Botanical gardens are found on each island. Tours of these gardens offer yet more enjoyment and education.

The Hawaii chapters of the Audubon Society (bird watching) and Sierra Club are active and sponsor classes, gatherings and field trips.

Horse breeding and horse riding are still popular, a leftover from Paniolo days. There are rodeos on each island.

Hawaii is home to "golf communities" or developments around golf courses/clubs. On Hawaii Island, Waikoloa is built around a golf course and the Hawaii Island Chamber of Commerce dubs its island "the Golf Island." Fourteen courses, some world class, host regular members, tournaments and visitors. Those designed by Robert Trent Jones, Sr. and Jr., include Mauna Kea Golf Course, Waikoloa Beach Golf Course, Waikoloa Village Golf Club and Kona Country Club. Fees range from twenty-five dollars at Hilo Municipal Golf Course (no sand traps!) to one hundred and fifty dollars at Francis H. Brown South and North Courses in Kohala. On Molokai, the Kaluakoi Resort is built next to the greens. These are just a few examples. Each island has championship courses either separate from or incorporated into residential developments.

Golf in Hawaii, a sport popular with local residents, has had a significant impact on tourism. As a major recreation activity, it competes with dining and shopping. Visitor research reports that tourists who come to golf spend more and tend to come even in recessionary times.

Oahu boasts an active golf community that numbers in the tens of thousands. There are 39 golf courses on Oahu, many strategically placed for access by tourists and residents alike.

Some courses are regarded as world class but whether public or private they are constantly crowded.[cxlvii] Check out www.island golf.com for information on all island golf.

So popular are the golf courses in Hawaii that their management has been subject to all sorts of underhanded procedures, including hacking the city computer system and petty bribes of staff members to obtain favorable tee times.[cxlviii]

However, golfing, despite its popularity, is politically controversial and constitutes an environmental indulgence that has come under fire.[cxlix] The venerable Ala Wai golf course adjacent to Waikiki is scheduled to close in 2000 in response to complaints re land use, water supply and environmental impact.[cl]

Fishing and hunting have been popular in Hawaii since the early settlements. Hawaii hosts the annual International Billfish Tournament. Deep-sea fishing enthusiasts travel from the Mainland and all over the world to bag "the big one." Hunting for wild pig and pheasant is also popular.

INDOOR

Hawaii isn't just beaches and spectacular scenery. The islands offer world-class entertainment – from local variety shows to large, national plays, musicals and variety shows.

Many small theaters were built during the sugar plantation hey-days, and several have been restored or are in the process of being restored. Some are used for performances of plays, concerts and lectures. Some still show movies. Many have historical societies involved in renovating and maintaining the buildings. They are always looking for new volunteers and funding. These small community theaters give interested parties an outlet for music and theater performances from Shakespeare to Neil Simon, from improv theatre to jazz jams.

Plays and movies are also shown at cultural centers and audi-
toriums on all islands. Productions from Honolulu, the Mainland
and Japan regularly tour Hawaii. If the show doesn't come to a
neighbor island, residents often take a small vacation to Oahu to
catch the ballet, opera or play. *Kamaaina* (local) prices are usually
offered at a discounted rate for air, room and car, which is one of
the advantages of being a resident. The Hawaii International Film
Festival (HIFF) is an eagerly anticipated annual event for residents of Hawaii, as well as visitors to the state. HIFF started as a
project of the East-West Center, and screened seven films from six
countries in 1981, its first year. It now has more than two dozen
screening sites on six Hawaiian Islands and draws an audience of
65,0000. Find more information at www.hiff.org.

The Merrie Monarch *hula* festival originated on the Big Island
37 years ago and now draws thousands of visitors from Oahu and
the Mainland.

Most districts also have community centers that provide space
for gatherings of people with mutual interests. A recent meeting
of "Seniors of Paradise" featured a talk on income tax, a potluck
lunch and announcements of interest groups including *hula*,
mahjong and managing your finances. Hawaii Island Senior
Institute (sponsored by University of Hawaii at Hilo) offers a lecture series at the University, including such topics as Hawaii's
economy, and a tour of the newly restored Palace Theater.

Hawaii is more than *hula* and slack key guitar[cli], but if you hap-
pen to enjoy the two, you are in the right place. There are shows
available in all the big hotels, as well as local watering holes and
private parties. Hawaiian, Jawaiian[clii], Hawaiian County—from
the Hawaiian cowboys, *paniolo*—and pop Hawaiian music can be
heard on the radio and television. The talent of local musicians
and singers is showcased here and on the Mainland. The Hawaii

entertainment community also brings international performers to the island for the enjoyment of tourists as well as local residents.

Ballroom dancing, line dancing and square dancing are all popular in Hawaii, and you will find many opportunities to learn or watch through groups, schools and community centers. *Hula halau*, or schools, offer instruction and entertainment on all islands. Numerous *hula* competitions are held on each island.

Hawaii also has its share of historical sites and museums. The history of Hawaii includes many nations and peoples. Specialty museums on each island are open to view homes of missionary families, whaling and sugar cane artifacts, fine arts and crafts including Hawaiian quilts and Hawaiian instruments, and homes and palaces of Hawaiian royalty. The state has a system of historical markers identifying points of interest. For attractions try the Hawaii Visitors and Convention Bureau (HVCB) website, and Puuhonua O Honaunau National Historic Park at www.nps.gov/puho. On Oahu, major sites include the Arizona Memorial, USS Missouri, Pearl Harbor, Bishop Museum and Iolani Palace.

On the Big Island of Hawaii, the Kona Historical Society Museum (www.ilhawaii.net/-khs), Kamuela Museum, Lyman House Memorial Museum and Hulihe'e Palace offer visitor and resident more historical points of interest. The Pacific Tsunami Museum in Hilo has a website with information about the museum and tsunamis. www.tsunami.org.

On Maui, The Baldwin Home and Museum in Lahaina is a popular museum and former home of a physician/missionary family. It is fully furnished in the period of the mid 1800s.

Life long learning is supported by the community colleges, adult schools and community/senior centers on each island. AARP on the Big Island has sponsored a weeklong "senior college" offering classes including art, hula, financial planning and creative writing. On Maui, a large center regularly has classes in swimming, aqua aerobics, calligraphy, ukulele and holiday cooking/ decorations.

Each island also offers opportunities for volunteer activities that may include working as a guide at a museum, answering phones at a shelter or cooking for fund-raising events.

New residents often take up or continue working in the arts – painting, writing, photography, theater and crafts of all sorts. Many of them report a special inspiration and creativity upon living in the islands. These hobbies often generate extra income for retirees who find receptive customers in the expanding visitor market.

Whatever and wherever your choice, there will be plenty of opportunities and activities to fill your time.

Chapter 7

Senior Palate in Paradise

"Life is uncertain. Eat dessert first."
Marie Callendar

Desserts, like the rest of the menu in Hawaii, represent the ethnic diversity of the population. Every culinary culture has its favorites. From Haupia (coconut) pudding to banana fritters Filipino style to mountain apple pie and macadamia cheesecake, from guava sherbet to Kona coffee ice cream Hawaii's cornucopia of desserts signals a sensual experience as tempting as the weather or the *hula*. Though usually served at the end of a meal, desserts are just the beginning of a gastronomique tour de force. In short, first time visitor or would be transplant, you are in for a treat in Hawaii.

Hawaii's diversity and ethnic traditions are nowhere so well expressed and so celebrated as in the many cuisines it offers to all palates. It is noteworthy that many "island dishes," even entire menus, originate, as do the people of Hawaii, from all over the world. For example, *Hawaii's BEST Cookbook on Fried Rice*, by George Yoshida, is a compilation of 31 recipes with local variations by local personages. Mr. Yoshida says,

"Here in Hawaii, we all love fried rice—the young and old, rich and poor, and interestingly everyone prepares it differently…be it

Japanese style, Chinese, Filipino, Portuguese, Korean, Hawaiian and even European, everyone does it with a unique kind of sizzle and Aloha."[cliii]

The author submitted a recipe, which is a wonderful illustration of the intermixing and assimilation of a basic dish of Chinese origin given a simultaneous local and cosmopolitan expression. Combine a single can of tuna, some chopped green onions, shoyu and three cups of cooked rice. He says it can feed an entire family for a cost of less than ninety-nine cents!

The family names, diverse and colorful, suggest how far this can go—Hispanic, Polynesian, Filipino, Hawaiian, Japanese and American and Chinese—all contributing to the integration and "ethnic" expression of culinary basics. This happens in Hawaii in architecture, fine art, dance, theater, medical practice, business and professional relations, religion and every form of human communication and social interaction. Stew, salad, or mixed plate—the diversity is what makes Hawaii Hawaii. Our favorites are as Hawaiian as the *hula*, as American as apple pie - chili fried rice and kalua pig.

In Hawaii virtually all the cuisines of the world are available for the taking (or making) by anyone with an appetite and access to a kitchen. As local food guru Ann Corum expresses it, "When people relocate to a new land, they bring with them little except for memories from home, which always include traditions, customs, and native foods. Races intermarry, creating a blend of customs and traditions in one family. This is what makes cultural traditions so rich."[cliv]

You may have experienced *manapua* in a Chinatown in a major city, but it was probably called a steamed pork bun. Food writer Joan Clarke explains that in Hawaii "Manapua [is a] …white steam wheat flour bun filled with chopped char siu (Chinese barbecue pork)."[clv]

Ms. Clarke also introduced us to the ubiquitous *huli huli* chicken: In Hawaiian, huli means to turn: huli huli chicken is turned many times over a kiawe grill …often sold as a fund-raiser …If you see a cloud of smoke emanating from a school or community center on weekends, it's likely to be a huli huli chicken sale."[clvi]

No gathering, celebration or funeral, is complete without *pupu.* "Pupu (pronounced poo poo) is what islanders call an appetizer, hors d'oeurve or munchie." [clvii]Some popular *pupu* in the islands are *manapua,* teriyaki meat sticks, macadamia nuts, fried won ton, sashimi, etc. Chips and salsa, guacamole, and local fruits and vegetables can be found on the snack table as well.

Honolulu, of course, is blessed with many fine restaurants, including family-style establishments, featuring Asian, Chinese, Mexican, French and traditional American menus. Hawaii also boasts restaurants serving a panoply of "local" dishes and specialties—*laulau, kalua* pig, *mahi mahi, kalbi (Korean style)ribs*—that constitute an adventure in exotic eating. "Mom & Pop" stands, serving up burger and fries, and saimin lunch counters abound, as do the common run of fast-food chain eateries. Quality and hygiene can vary from place to place and caution is advised.

Luau are an experience to behold. They are not unlike Texas bar-b-ques, Louisiana fish fries and New England clambakes, each featuring its ethnic and local variations on a theme of feasting. Wherever you are from and whatever your taste, Hawaii can accommodate your preferences, taste buds and budget. Poi, a luau staple, and Hawaii's answer to grits, is steamed and mashed taro. As one old timer had it, visitors are advised to try poi at least once so they can bad mouth it with authority.

Food festivals, fairs and "tastings" are part of the many activities and events that draw people to Hawaii. If you have enjoyed Julia Child or the Ragin' Cajun, you will enjoy local celebrity chef

Sam Choy's cooking show, restaurant and many books on Hawaiian Regional Cuisine. Other celebrity chefs include Roy Yamaguchi, Amy Ota and Chef Ellman of Maui Taco. A short list of Hawaiian food books is included as Table 7-1.

One would assume that Hawaii's location in the mid-Pacific, surrounded by vast expanses of ocean, would yield a cornucopia of seafood products. Accordingly, fish should be of virtually unlimited availability, and the price of fish should be moderate. Unfortunately, this is not so, for a variety of reasons. Many species are quite expensive, from the popular *mahi mahi* to *ahi* tuna, marlin, shark, swordfish and snapper, as well as several species of shellfish. Many locals fish from banks and bridges to supplement their market purchases. Fish markets offer the best buy, but supermarkets tend to offer the best quality.

As we consider eating out is part of an active lifestyle, we are happy to share our adventures with potential residents of Hawaii. This guide is not complete and favors modestly priced establishments. We felt no need to include hotel dining or "high ticket" restaurants as they are well advertised. We have tried to include a variety of places that locals and experienced travelers frequent. We feature restaurants, cafes, and hotel dining rooms that favor and cater to retirees, seniors and elders.

Except for a select few dishes, such as *laulau (banana leaves) chicken* and *kalua (roast)* pig, "local" food does not really have deep roots in Hawaiian culture. What most people refer to as local food is eaten in "plate lunches," popular everywhere in Hawaii. It consists of dishes such as fried chicken, beef stew, teriyaki pork and breaded *mahi mahi*; much of it is deep-fried. A plate lunch is invariably accompanied by two carbohydrates, usually rice and a macaroni or potato-macaroni salad. Another local favorite is called the *loco moco*—that's a hamburger patty over rice topped with a fried egg and brown gravy. Warning: Don't go local if you're counting calories or looking for "heart-healthy" food! Another word to the wise: many chicken dishes are prepared with chicken thighs instead of breast meat. If you have a preference, ask before ordering. Burgers are, as elsewhere, routinely over-cooked so unless you favor really charred char-burgers be sure to specify your order.

Here is a brief sampling of restaurants we have known and loved divided into "occasion" or vacation splurge, family fare and "burgers, fries and pizza pies". We have added bakeries and vegetarian spots since we enjoy them and hope you will too.

TOP TEN RESTAURANTS FOR SENIORS*
*Where you would take your Mom for a treat!

OCCASION PLACES

1. GAYLORDS at Kilohana, 3-2-87 Kaumaulii Hwy, Lihue, Kauai 808/245-9593 – Located in the lovely Kilohana plantation, the building is a former residence converted to a complex of galleries and restaurant serving lunch, dinner and Sunday brunch in a courtyard setting. A bit pricey, but a dandy place for Mother's Day, etc. The champagne flowed and the service was excellent.

2. The CROUCHING LION INN, Windward Oahu, 51-666 Kamehameha Hwy, Kaaawa; 237-8511. Serving lunch and dinner, the Crouching Lion Inn is a "view" attraction as well as a popular spot for tour buses. Try to arrive at an off-hour.

3. NANI MAU GARDEN RESTAURANT, 421 Makalika Street, Big Island, just south of Hilo off Volcano Highway #11. 959-3541. The restaurant, featuring a lunch buffet, has an arresting view of the 20 acre garden. At a recent visit at Thanksgiving the menu featured

three scrumptious entrees and a generous selection of salads, side dishes and desserts at $17.95. This included a tip and admission to the gardens, a popular tourist stop.

4. HOTEL MOLOKAI, Molokai Lunch - salads and sandwiches $6.50 - $7.50, daily specials. Popularly priced for visitors and locals. Good fish dishes, salads and desserts. Dinners include rice or french fries, vegetable medley and soup or salad - $11.00 - $19.00. Local musicians play for dinner. We found it to be a restful beachfront setting.

5. HOTEL HANA-MAUI, main dining room, Maui 248-8211 The dining room is the only fine dining in Hana. The beautiful, soothing, luxurious surroundings are considered worth the drive. Prices are equally luxurious and not quite so soothing. Food is Pacific Rim-Hawaiian Regional. Service is good to excellent.

6. THE KONA BEACH RESTAURANT, 75-5660 Palani Rd. in the Kona Beach King Kamehameha Hotel serves breakfast, lunch and dinner buffets. Rated "Best Bets – Best Buffets" by *Hawaii the Big Island*, King Kam is a local occasion outing on the west side of the Big Island. We heartily agree. The selections vary day by day.

7. THE TERRACE at the Mauna Kea Beach Hotel (Big Island - Kohala) 882-722 is the home of a popular daily buffet luncheon served on the terrace with a view of Mauna Kea's wonderful beach. It also has a very pleasant daily buffet breakfast. We still recall fondly a memorable scallops in cream sauce dish we ate there.

8. ROY'S KAHANA BAR & GRILL (669-6999) and ROY'S NICOLINA (669-5000) in Lahaina, Maui offer Hawaiian Regional/Eurasian food. These restaurants are next door to each other with Nicolina described as a quieter, more intimate environment.

9. KOA HOUSE GRILL, 65-1144 Mamalahoa Hwy, Waimea, Big Island. 885-2088 Formerly "Cattleman's Steakhouse," Koa House Grill features Hawaii Regional cuisine in a charming dining room. There is a nice salad bar selection. Service and food are excellent. We found lunch to be the best value ($8.00 − 12.00), especially if you skip desserts which tend to be expensive.

10. TOP OF WAIKIKI, Honolulu, Oahu. 2270 Kalakaua Ave. 923-3877 A revolving restaurant. The view is magnificent and worth the price of the well prepared basic dishes, especially at sunset.

FAMILY FARE

Many retirees will seek out the family oriented establishments many of whom accommodate elders and offer discounts to seniors.

1. BUZZ'S ORIGINAL STEAK HOUSE, 413 Kawailoa Rd., Kailua, Windward Oahu serving steak and fish, is still popular in the neighborhood. 261-4661 Buzz's has a mostly local clientele and moderate prices - reservations are advised. Also in Pearl City, 98-751 Kuahoa Pl. 487-6465.

2. CHUM'S, 1900 Main St., Wailuku, Maui 244-1000 Chum's is located in a Wailuku mini-mall and offers "large portions" of "local-style food". It's a basic place to eat cheap, so regulars rarely leave disappointed.

3. HAWAIIAN STYLE CAFE, Waimea, Big Island on the highway across from Parker Square. 885-4295 Recommended by the local moving company. The breakfast and lunches are HUGE! Omelets include potatoes and pancakes. $5.50 average.

4. KEN'S HOUSE OF PANCAKES, 1730 Kamehameha Ave., Hilo, Big Island 935-8711 open 24 hours. American/local -

Breakfast, lunch, dinner. Senior portions. All day breakfast including macadamia nut pancakes - $4.95 Lunch includes hamburgers, grilled mahimahi, chicken, etc. Sandwiches about $6.00, dinners about $8-9.00. Cuisines include Chinese, Filipino, Hawaiian and Japanese dishes. Located minutes from the Hilo airport Ken's is frequented by those arriving and departing as well as local office workers and laborers. Friendly service; moderate prices.

5. REUBEN'S MEXICAN FOOD, 336 Kamehameha Ave., Hilo, Big Island 961-2552 Mexican (Hawaii Tribune Herald best Mexican restaurant). All types of enchiladas and Mexican specialties. Enchiladas (beef) $8.00 with rice and beans. Flautas, quesadillas, and grilled garlic fla-vored mahi-mahi round out an authentic Mexican menu. Real margaritas and tasty guacamole. We vote Reuben's collection of sombreros best in the Islands. Watch out for the "lava" sauce.

6. HANAPEPE CAFÉ, 3830 Hanapepe Road, Hanapepe, Kauai 335-5011. French-Italian-Vegetarian, Breakfast, lunch, dinner. Fresh baked goods and local produce. The brunch specials are clever and delicious.

7. LIHUE BARBEQUE INN, 2982 Kress Street, Lihue, Kauai is a locally recommended favorite. 245-2921 Lunch includes soup, a beverage, fresh bread, an entree such as teriyaki chicken sandwich and dessert for $6.95. Open for breakfast, lunch and dinner. It is also recom-mended by *Hawaii Kauai Underground Guide* [clviii].

8. SCRUFFLES Restaurant, 1438 Kilauea Ave., Hilo, Big Island 935-6664. Family coffee shop-style with a menu featuring a variety of cuisines including burgers and sandwiches, Japanese and American specials, soups and salads. This restaurant's clean surroundings, varied

menu and generally good food earn it a spot in "Top Family Restaurants" by *Hawaii the Big Island*. * Next door is a bakery/espresso/sushi bar with excellent eat in or out selections. The clientele includes many seniors and elders from all ethnic groups. A favorite for ladies' luncheons.

9. Buffet 100, Honolulu, Oahu, with more than 100 items opened a second location at Westridge Shopping Center recently. The first location at the Ward Warehouse has been offering breakfast, lunch ($7.95) and dinner ($12.95) (Sunday brunch $10.95)) for two years, featuring Mandarin-style recipes and local favorites, serving teriyaki beef, barbecue chicken, curry stews, chicken katsu[clix], Chinese dishes, salad bar and dessert. Diners over 62 years can take advantage of a 15 percent savings.

10. MANAGO HOTEL DINING ROOM, in the Manago Hotel, Captain Cook, Big Island, 323-2642 American, with Japanese sides. Dinners include pork chops, ahi, mahimahi or steak. Served family style. Excellent value. The clientele is local residents, travelers from other islands, and tourists from just about everywhere. Cash only. Dinners about $8.00; dishes vary daily.

BURGERS, FRIES AND PIZZA PIES

To our lasting shame we offer the following fast-food, pick-up and take-out establishments serving foods you would be wise to by-pass for the sake of your diet. But if you're exploring Hawaii or if you're headed to or from the beach or golf course, these on-the-run eateries provide roadside sustenance until you can get back to your frig. or locate a proper food source.

1. CHARLEY'S, Keaau Shopping Center, Big Island— sandwiches, burgers and sometimes pizza on the small

patio. Charlies offers a real burger, larapin' bar-b-que beans and good cole slaw. (Ask for your burger the way you want it. Sometimes the cook gets distracted with football or boxing and medium becomes well done.) It is a sports bar and features live music most nights of the week. A good stop on the way to Volcanoes National Park just off HWY 11.

2. CAFÉ IL MONDO, 45-3636-A Mamane Street, Honokaa, Big Island 775-7711 Italian Pizzeria and Coffee Bar. Pizza $7.50–$17.25, Sandwiches $3.95 - $4.50, Lasagna with salad and garlic bread $7.95. Also Calzone and espresso. The owner is a musician and his tapes play as background. Beautiful flower paintings mix with fresh flower arrangements to provide a delightful eating experience. Sometimes there is live music, but the schedule is irregular. We found the inventive pizzas (pesto, four cheese, veggie, etc.) to be among the best anywhere in the Islands.

3. KUA'AINA SANDWICH, 66-214 Kamehameha Hwy, Haleiwa, Oahu. 637-606, Haleiwa Legendary North Shore hamburger counter. Excellent burgers. New location in midtown Honolulu - Ward Village Shops, 1116 Auahi St. (Kamakee St.) Staffed by local youths, be sure to get their attention before they inhale!

4. DUANE'S ONO CHAR BURGER, Kauai. A rustic roadside stand between Lihue and Hanalai. No credit cards, but low prices and locally recommended. Watch out for the catsup that comes with it if you don't ask.

5. BILLY BOB'S PARK 'N PORK, South Kona, Big Island, (323-3371) Hours are 5-9 for dinner only. BBQ. Voted Kona's best BBQ in Captain Cook just south of MM111.

We agree. Ribs and beef were succulent. Either restrain yourself or take a supply of Tums. Dinner $7 - $11.

6.   ZIPPY'S, usually open 24 hours, Honolulu, Oahu (local - over 20 locations on Oahu) and Denny's (national) are part of coffee shop chains. What they lack in glamour, they make up for with reasonable prices, good selection and senior discounts. Zippy's also has Dr. Shintani's Hawaii Diet main dishes.[clx]

DENNY'S in Kona (Big Island) is part of the coffee shop chain with an augmented menu, senior discounts, and a great view of Kona Bay.

7.   CHEESEBURGER IN PARADISE, 811 Front St., Lahaina, Maui. Grab a table on the deck over the water for a great view of Lahaina Bay. There can be a long wait (especially at sunset) and there is not much selection for vegetarians. But the view is unsurpassed and the prices are budget for Lahaina.

8.   BRICK OVEN PIZZA, Kalaheo, Kauai 332-8561. The hearth-baked pizzas are "very ono" at this friendly eatery. Brick Oven Pizza is located en route to Waimea Canyon. Considered a bit pricey, it also a reliably "good to go-back-to place."

9.   BOSTON'S NORTH END PIZZA BAKERY, Oahu has locations in Honolulu, Kailua, Kaimuki, Kaneohe and Kapolei. Many consider this chain a great value and "best on the island." The spinach garlic pie is a favorite.

10.   On the Big Island, CAFÉ PESTO could be called an occasion/pizza place. With locations in Hilo (308 Kamehameha Ave. 969-6640) and Kawaihae (Kawaihae Shopping Center 882-1071), these smoke-free restaurants, serve delicious pasta and gourmet pizza, salads

and excellent desserts. A bit pricey, but the service is friendly and the fare is scrumptious

HONORABLE MENTION

On the Big Island at Kainaliu (Aloha Theater Complex), The ALOHA CAFÉ (322-3383) is known for its wonderful breakfasts, generous burgers and great view from the relaxing outdoor patio. Delectable pastries are available to complement your mocha or latte.

BAKERIES and VEGETARIAN

Worthy of inclusion also are local bakeries offering local variations on virtually everything from everywhere. Don't presume, e.g., some Japanese owned bakeries create fine French pastry; others combine Mexican desserts with American or Filipino specialties. Most offer "local" items and have a "local" following willing to boast about their favorite dish. We include three "veggie" restaurants for those would-be herbivores looking for more than a green salad. Enjoy!

1. KANEMITSU BAKERY, Molokai 553-5855 - a real bakery serving breakfast and lunch - also take out. Budget. People fly in to shop at this bakery. YUM!

2. BUNS IN THE SUN, Kona, Big Island 326-2774, Lanihau Shopping Center off Palani Road. Breakfast and lunch. Some sources say "avoid the biscuits and gravy; they taste like plastic." The breads and pastries are fresh and belie the reputation of the biscuits and gravy. $3 - $8.

3. NAPOLEAN'S, Honolulu, Oahu. Napoleon's is the bakery branch of Zippy's. They have delicious pies, cakes, malasadas, empanadas, Danish pastries, donuts, etc. You

will find one everywhere on Oahu. Reliably good; moderate prices.

4. In Hilo, check out SCRUFFLES for all kine goodies. They also have take out lunches, snacks, sushi platters; catering is available. The lemon tart is very ono! See #8 in Family Fare.

5. TEX DRIVE INN, Honokaa, Big Island, is famous for their hot malasadas. (Malasadas are Portuguese donuts without a hole.) They now have filled malasadas with cream, lilikoi and other fillings. Sandwiches, breakfast and plate lunches round out the menu.

6. ANNA MILLER'S, Pearlridge Center, Oahu 487-2421, is a 24-hour coffee shop in Aiea serving fast food and burgers. It is known for its great strawberry and banana cream pies. Generally receiving a "so so" rating for food in general, Anna Miller's won the Hale Aina Award for Best Dessert.

7. KILAUEA BAKERY & PAU HANA PIZZA, Kong Lung Center, Kilauea, Kauai 828-2020 This establishment – bakery/coffee shop/pizzeria – is rated "the best pizza in the state" by Zagat. We found it rivals but does not surpass Café Il Mondo in Honokaa.

8. THE VEGAN RESTAURANT, ("Incredibly Delicious Vegetarian Cuisine.") 115 Baldwin Ave., Paia, Maui 579-9144 Small but excellent vegan, so unique even carnivores would love it. They serve sandwiches, salads and soup for lunch. The dinner menu includes curry veggies, garlic veggies and grilled polenta. Prices $3.00 - $10.00. Hours 11 am – 9 pm.

9. PAPAYA'S NATURAL GOURMET, Kauai Village, Kapa, Kauai 823-0190. Crunchy granola types in search of natural foods with flavor frequent this self-serve coffee

shop/health food store in Kapaa; it fills a need for more vegetarian eateries on Kauai but fails to provide enough variety.

10.   MOCHA JAVA CAFÉ, Ward Center, Honolulu, Oahu 591-9023

Locals love to meet for business or pleasure at this Ward Centre Vegetarian/Health Fooder and nibble on "good morning food", "yummy curry veggie burgers" or homemade soup and bread topped off with the "best chocolate espresso milk shake"; too bad it's not open all the time."[clxi]

Vegetarian restaurants are few, but many health food stores have added kitchens and take out services with delicious and healthy smoothies, soups and salads (for example, Island Naturals and Abundant Life in Hilo). They have a few tables or counter space for customer dining. Service is strictly self-reliance.

Two of our favorites deserve inclusion in the honorable mention category:

Plate lunch offerings – on wagons sometimes referred to as "roach coaches" or in small deli-type or open air cafes – are standard fare throughout the islands. Sometimes they are referred to as Bento, a variation on the carry out lunch pail carried by laborers and plantation workers of the past. Our favorites are the lunch plate offerings at the Papaaloa Store (and post office) Complex on the Big Island. This off the beaten path "general store" features a different plate lunch each day (served with rice, mac salad, or tossed greens) for local clientele. Generous portions; authentic local food; modest prices. Drinks, side dishes, and treats are available. We live a short walk away, but local workers and residents drive 10 or more miles for lunch.[clxii]

Another noteworthy display of "ethnic" cuisine served cafeteria style at modest prices may be found at the East-West Center located on the east side of the University of Hawaii, Manoa campus. A genuine ethnic stew prepared for student bodies from Asia and around the world. While you are there enjoy a view of the Manoa Stream, Koi fish aswimming and the mixed-plate architecture of the campus.

Open-air markets often sell food on the side of the road at good prices. Look for fruit smoothies, tamales, sushi, huli huli chicken, whateva. But be cautious re freshness and food handling practices.

Unfortunately there is no useful restaurant guide for seniors and elders. Part of this is due to the fact that restaurants cater to tourists and are priced and presented accordingly. However, there is a guide to smoke free dining available through the Health Department.

Tips for retirees:

Look for a local following

Ask for senior discounts or small portions

Don't believe all rave reviews

Review the menu, usually posted, before you enter

Before planning our trips to various islands, we looked through general and restaurant guides including Hidden Hawaii, Kauai Underground Guide, Zagat Survey and others. Take a look at our recommended reading and enjoy!

Chapter 8

Fruits of Our Labors:
Our Top Ten Places to Retire

"If your heart is in your dreams no request is too extreme."[clxiii] *J. Cricket (1940)*

Hawaii is the one of the world's most promising and rewarding retirement sites. Despite crowding and congestion in urban areas, spotty social services and prices that can be frightening, Hawaii offers good values and remains one of the finest recreation and retirement sites available anywhere.

The fiftieth state will continue to be attractive well into this century, although badly burdened by the overlapping effects of population increase, economic development and environmental depletion. The part played by Hawaii's lingering desirability and affordability combined will become even more prominent in coming years as the local population ages and swells. The island population will become older, more affluent and more demanding of health care and local services.

Retirement is both rewarding as well as traumatic for many people. So, why make it worse by uprooting your household, spouse or family and moving to a volcanic archipelago subject to tsunamis, landslides, hurricanes, earthquakes, drenching rains, and scorching sun, outrageous prices and dubious politics? The answer will carry us beyond the scope of our inquiry. However we are now in a position to provide provisional answers to some of the basic questions posed at the outset. These questions, and our "top ten" list of desirable retirement sites, are the fruits of our labors. The answers have far-reaching implications for life in Hawaii in the 21st century. We offer provisional answers and a list of favorites for the reader's consideration, to wit:

1) Is Hawaii a good place to retire? That depends on your health, wealth and tolerance for ethnic diversity and, of course, "stranded" on an isolated group of large rocks in the middle of a vast ocean, your affinity for warm and sunny days.

2) Is Hawaii retiree friendly? On balance, we find that transplant retirees do fare well and are welcome—even encouraged—despite the oddities of their generation and their lack of knowledge or concern for local issues and indigenous customs.

3) Will my retirement income be sufficient for Hawaii's prices? Yes, any amount over $24,000 will make it possible. But $24,000 is a recommended minimum. Poverty in Hawaii does not mean quite the same thing as it does on the Mainland. Even those in poverty, one may argue, suffer less in the islands than in the cities of the U.S. and elsewhere. We have met retirees who claim to live comfortable healthy lives on far less but any amount over $24,000, or any supplemental income or growth in your savings and investments, will make a comfortable retirement more likely. We recommend a $30,000 annual income to provide a modest cushion and margin for error even at today's prices. If you have an income of $30,000 or more, you can afford cable TV and an occasional trip to the Mainland!

4) Should I invest in Hawaii as I retire to Hawaii?

Hawaii is and will continue to yield profits and secondary returns for the deft and well-informed investor. As the recession of the '90s began to be felt in Hawaii many were in denial and were slow to adjust and adapt. When we purchased a home in 1992 we would have cautioned retirees regarding investing in Hawaii's corporations, public bonds, and new ventures. The '90s were clearly recessionary, and had a devastating effect on the total economy, a "bust" by almost any standards. Although the dark clouds of over-development and over-crowding that portend social problems are on the horizon, the long-term investment prospects through the first half of the 21st century are fair to good, especially in housing, diversified agriculture and new technology. Tourism is still branching out, with ecotours, sport, health and wellness activities, and conventions. But the traditional tourist markets, like golf and deep-sea fishing, are well developed and very competitive. Be cautioned regarding real estate speculation, tourism and travel service schemes, and a litany of investment scams, some of which target retirees and the elderly.

5)   Will I be able to buy my favorite brands and lines of merchandise? Probably yes, plus tax, shipping and handling, which add about 10% on average. All the major U. S. chains from McDonalds to Sears, Safeway and Wal-Mart are present, as are Sony, Aiwa, Samsung and many of the players in the global market place. For better or worse Hawaii is thus an international marketplace, a hub of goods and services from the Pacific Rim and the West Coast of the U.S. and Canada. Certain imported items, like wine, olives, and cheese, are unavailable or in limited supply on the rural islands. Occasional shortages

of things like produce and paper goods occur even on Oahu during shipping or docking strikes which in turn provoke gouging, e.g. gas prices, and hoarding e.g. toilet paper.

6)   Will I find adequate health care? It depends on what you mean by health care, and whether access to it is a part of a health care system or service. On Oahu health care at all levels is available but at a price; on the rural islands services may be available, but with a delay for special services such as organ transplants and major surgery. Until the last few years, expensive diagnostic equipment was centrally located on Oahu. Recently neighbor island facilities have been purchasing MRI and CAT scan equipment. This will reduce inter-island travel for these tests.

7)   What about elder care? The level of care is generally good, but not sufficient to meet future levels of need. This is roundly acknowledged by state agencies, service providers, planner, and educators. Traditionally, families in Hawaii have cared for their own elders. This has changed because of the increased number of working couples unable to provide these services at home. New residents without family face the same problem. An attempt to bridge the "eldercare gap" can be found in the independent health care facilities and other forms of private care. The Adult Residential Care Home (ARCH) providers are available to care for small numbers, usually 2-6 residents, of elders. Adult Residential Care Homes provide shelter, supervision and care, but do not offer medical or skilled nursing services. Unlike the SNF (skilled nursing facilities), adult residential care homes are not licensed to receive reimbursement under

Medicare and Medicaid programs. More information may be obtained through the Hawaii State Department of Health. State of Hawaii, Hawaii District Health Office, Adult Residential Care Homes, 75 Aupuni Street R.105 Hilo, 96720, (808) 974-6006.

Some persons turn to adult day care or private nurses as interim providers for those suffering from Alzheimer's, stroke, or other disease that plague the aging population. In the end, any living arrangement requiring professional care is expensive and often bewildering to patient and family caregiver alike.

8) Should I be concerned about "Rock Fever"? Yes, you would do well to anticipate the socio-psychological effect of relocation to an island that may be thousands of miles from any major landmass and characterized by ethnic mixtures heretofore unfamiliar to you. "Rock Fever" can take many forms and can, if you don't listen to your own feelings, lead to feelings of isolation, homesickness, loneliness and serious depression.

9) Will I find like-minded people? Unless you are a left-handed iconoclast with no life and zero personality, bent on a hermitage in a rift zone cave, you will almost certainly find kindred spirits in the islands. Cliques of every stripe and kind exist throughout Hawaii. New interest groups emerge on a regular basis. For example we found more drummers per capita on the Big Isle than in the San Francisco Bay Area.

Throughout Hawaii, awareness of ethnic history and identity are keen, but Hawaii and retirement are both rich opportunities for making new friends and exploring new interests and hobbies. A little effort and a measure of *aloha* will carry you a long way. Think of it as personal outreach or as just getting acquainted. Grandparents from any place and any culture always enjoy swapping stories about grandchildren (*mo'opuna* in Hawaiian). Also, retirees everywhere like to talk about where they've been and what they have done. Tall tales, fish stories, and war anecdotes are no less common in Hawaii than any elder enclave.

10) What is it like to grow old in Hawaii? As elsewhere, aging is as much a matter of attitude as annual rings etched into your body. Aging is inevitable; growing old is not. In the islands, life can be more fun for the elderly just because Hawaii is Hawaii. Hawaii is warmer, more beautiful, and the culture is probably more accepting and supportive of aging persons than wherever you came from. Also, there are and will be more elder persons to grow old with than in most places. If you are fortunate enough to grow old in Hawaii you will likely do so in a benign environment. You will likely find yourself drawn into what locals call "talk story," an island version of gab, gossip and oral history.

Whatever your choice, make it an informed one even if it is predicated on emotions. Create your own network of contacts and resources as well as your own vision of Hawaii. Retirement to Hawaii can be an adventure beyond any you have had before. Leaving home and family, friends and familiar places can be an exciting growth experience, even if it occurs in your later years when your memory dims and you move a little slower. Living in Hawaii, just residing or passing time here, can be a wonderful daily tonic to those with senses that are still keen and minds that are still open.

In the course of researching and writing this book we visited each island and drove (or hiked) to areas beyond the paved roads and electric power grid. We have been rewarded for our efforts by selecting a home and retirement site for ourselves from among the many villages, towns and subdivisions. Our choice was a small "sugar cane" village (population around 500) on the Hamakua Coast, bracketed by streams and surrounded by agricultural and pasture land with Mauna Kea looming majestically in the background. What looked like a sleepy do-nothing, go nowhere cluster of old and new housing was, as we got to know it, a beehive of residents going about their business and tending their families.

OUR TOP TEN CHOICES

As we visited each of the major islands we attempted to assess them from the point of view of a prospective retiree seeking a second or permanent home, willing and able to relocate.

Our research plan took us to secluded villages, housing projects in process (some with few houses in place), backwoods cabins, and up-scale sub-divisions, to gated communities and "lost" hovels, even tree houses, hidden in gulches or located deep in rain forests. From our research, visits and inquiries come our own favorites, our "top ten" places to retire in Hawaii.

Out of these travels we selected what we perceived to be desirable, affordable and accessible to retirees still mobile and in relatively good health. The choices were clear in some cases obscure in others. Sometimes the place just had a "feel," an ambience, a mood, a lifestyle, call it what you will, that led us to recommend it.

Our choices begin with the area we hold most dear-the one we chose for ourselves as "right for us" and can recommend to others with the provisos and caveats previously articulated.

1. <u>Hamakua District</u> Villages of Papaaloa-Laupahoehoe, halfway up the Hamakua Coast (52 continuous miles of agricultural and pastoral land punctuated by a score of villages and camps running from Hilo to Waipio Valley), we "discovered" the village of Papaaloa, literally sitting on bluffs overlooking the ocean. Its low elevation was an ideal spot for a small experimental citrus, macadamia nut and tropical fruit orchard. We enjoy good roads and highway access, a spectacular ocean view and a still intact rural setting. Within walking distance we have a general store, post office, library, gym, tennis courts, swimming pool, churches and missions, a gas/convenience store, senior nutrition center and weekend farmer's market, much like architect Oda's vision of genuine contemporary Hawaiian villages, but absent (perhaps thankfully) a MacDonalds franchise. Laupahoehoe Elementary and High School, home to the Laupahoehoe Seasiders, is a center of community activity. Laupahoehoe Beach Park is a short drive or healthy hike away.

2. <u>Oahu; North Shore</u> Situated on the North shore of Oahu (roughly from La'ie and Kahuku to the Haleiwa-Waialua) is a relatively undeveloped area with many beach parks and rugged inland areas in between. The area is still accessible, still affordable, with services and infrastructure but not yet overrun, except on those awesome surf days and during "festivals." It is still one of Oahu's most out of the way places, and it retains the charm and beauty that characterize rural Hawaii. If this is your destination don't tarry, as the desirable housing sites are being gobbled up.

3. <u>Waimea/Kamuela, Big Island of Hawaii</u> Located in the uplands of the Big Island ranch country (2,500 feet), is a mix of traditional Hawaiian and upscale contemporary living. Cool and often rainy, it affords unparalleled views of the Kona-Kohala area. In a recent study it was designated the tenth most desirable place to live in the U.S.[clxiv] We rank it the third most desirable place to retire in

Hawaii. It features a local playhouse, a theatre, a small airport, several nice restaurants, golf courses, several churches, ranches and rodeos, an active art community, and senior center and county nutrition program, even meals on wheels. All services are available, including the North Hawaii Community Hospital, now fully staffed and functioning. And yes, there is a MacDonalds!

4. Kailua-Lanikai, Oahu For tropical suburban life at its best, this area, though choked by commuter traffic during the week and sometimes overrun by beach goers on holidays, is a near perfect suburb. A 30-40 minute commute takes you to Honolulu, Waikiki and the University of Hawaii. Many restaurants, social services, shops, parks and churches are available.

5. Honolulu, Manoa Valley (Oahu) If it's proximity to a university library (University of Hawaii, Manoa) and a conventional neighborhood you seek, Manoa is tops in our estimation. Housing is expensive but services and shops are widely available, and the main arterial (University Avenue) ties to the freeway and onto Waikiki and downtown Honolulu. Public transportation and senior services are readily available. The morning showers in the upper valley keep the air fresh, fragrant and cool. Manoa Valley's strong neighborhood board was a big plus for us. This provides for direct community input, and local oversight and responsibility for local issues. The valley community offers condominiums, single-family dwellings, apartments and *ohana*, many of which are sought after by students and faculty. In Manoa you will find a retinue of active retirees and long-term residents, many affiliated with one of the many departments or research centers of the University of Hawaii. If there is a retired intelligentsia in Hawaii it is focused in Manoa Valley and surrounding residential area.

6. Waikoloa Village North Kona, on the Big Island of Hawaii If you can afford it, and especially if you are a golfer, this made-for-retirees planned community development located south of

Waimea and six miles inland from the North Kohala coast is made for you. Landscaped around a golf course, the project includes shops, fire and police services and many view units. Composed of "cookie cutter" town house and apartment units, the uniform construction and color scheme will be a bore to some and a comfort to others. This area is also conveniently located near Keahole airport just north of Kona, with daily flights to the Mainland. A short drive to the Kona-Kohala Coast takes you to the opulent Waikaloa Village Resort, sometimes referred to as a "Disneyland for adults," and some of the best beaches (Hapuna, Spencer) in the islands.

7. Wailuku, Maui (central) This community is the county seat, near the airport. Housing is reasonably priced in this area and medical services, recreation and entertainment are conveniently located. An active senior community of Mainland transplants, Canadian "snow birds" and retirees from Maui and Oahu are already in residence. For physical and mental stimulation Maui Community College and Maui Arts and Culture Center present classes, performances (music and drama), art exhibitions and community events. Wailuku is near H.P. Baldwin Beach Park one of the most scenic beaches on Maui.

8. Hana, Maui If back-roads living is your preference, Hana may be the place in your dreams. The legendary road to Hana, always under construction or in need of it, crosses some 63 bridges and 53 miles of rugged coastal beauty, waterfalls and rain forests. Suggested driving time is two and a half hours, but if you make this trip in less than four hours you probably failed to smell the flowers and appreciate the scenery. While remote by automobile, Hana boasts an "airport," better described as a landing strip, for small aircraft. There is also a port, long since abandoned, and a landing-launching facility for small boats. Long on natural beauty but short on restaurants and services Hana is the most iso-

lated town on one of the most isolated land masses on earth, and its reputation as a backwater is rock solid. There is but one hotel and one general store (Hasagawa's); the principal occupations are farming and diversified agriculture. Hana's principal amenity, if you will, is open space combined with low population density.

9. <u>Hanalei and the Napali Coast, Kauai</u> For sheer beauty in a rural, rustic and remote locale, Hanalei and the Napali coast (accessible only by boat and highly touted for its campgrounds and trails), on the North shore of Kauai, are still there to be enjoyed. A 45-minute, 30-mile drive takes you back to Lihue and "civilization." In spite of the beating and havoc wrought by hurricane Iwa in 1982 and hurricane Iniki in 1992, this coastal area is rural Hawaii personified. Construction is expensive and services are sparse. The backwoods agricultural and rural village ambience have been maintained in spite of attempts at gentrification and development.

10. <u>Puna-Pahoa, Big Island of Hawaii</u> The Puna-Pahoa area is prime for the owner-builder or virtual homesteader. (Virtual homesteading refers to the independent "pioneers" who use solar, wind and propane power rather than hooking up to "the grid." Their water supply may also be off-grid, relying on rainwater catchment technology. See Chapter 4) The still affordable region (one to five acres for $5,000 to $20,000) has open spaces, a rugged beauty born of rejuvenated lava flows, and a country ambience that appeals to many retirees. Perhaps as many as 5,000 retired persons are already there being absorbed into an evolving community. The population in this region may increase rapidly in the next two decades, abetted by stand-alone habitats and off-grid technology. Hilo lies some 20-30 miles north of Pahoa and is the commercial and employment hub for many of the residents of the Puna district.

Other areas deserve **honorable mention** as desirable for seniors and/or retirees.

Molokai's south shore, from Kaunakakai to Halawa Valley, is still uncluttered, largely unspoiled and sparsely populated. Molokai's south shore will appeal to others as it did to us. "For Sale By Owner" signs are visible along the roads running through several "camps," as are second-generation condos. Roads are fair; services are few. Beaches are pristine, and fishing and snorkeling are world class! This "backwater" place is ideal for "backwater people," and a popular respite for island residents, especially from Oahu.

South Kona, Big Island of Hawaii From South Kona to Ocean View near South Point one will find an emerging community of flower farms, coffee plantations, and diversified agriculture suitable for retirees. Hawaii Ocean View Estates, a subdivision about 35 miles south of Kona, is a growing community with limited infrastructure but unlimited views of the ocean providing year round spectacular sunsets. Note that in this area vog may be a problem for those with respiratory ailments.

Lihue/Kapaa, Kauai This area includes Lihue (county seat) and is located convenient to the airport, shopping, services and entertainment. Apartments, houses and condominiums provide housing options for seniors. Nearby Kapaa is a mix of tourist accommodations, small condominium complexes and subdivisions. Most of this area is on or near the beach.

Molokai, west end Condominiums and large building parcels are available in this relatively undeveloped region. The area is arid and desert-like, but utilities and water are available to most sites. Papohaku Beach offers the best snorkeling on Molokai, perhaps the best in the islands, perhaps the best in the world. If you're looking for a remote area to build your dream home, this may be it.

Hawaii Kai, East Oahu For sheer presence of amenities and upscale living, Hawaii Kai, with access to transportation, many services, intact infrastructure, a prepackaged calendar of recreation and social events, is a well-established retirement community that is still evolving and expanding. If assisted living is what you prefer or require, this top of the line residential community merits consideration

Hilo, the biggest little city in Hawaii (on the Big Island), Hilo Town is home to a sizable population of retired people living in apartments, condominiums, conventional residences and ohana (attached but independent units). Activities for seniors are many and varied. With several large senior centers, medical and transportation services, churches and theaters, it is a good choice for those with mobility problems. Real estate values continue to favor buyers of existing residential housing, perhaps the best buys in the residential market anywhere in Hawaii. Joe Correa, a realtor with 20 years of experience on the Big Island,[clxv] advised us that one could purchase a 3 bedroom/2 bath home in Hilo starting at approximately $140,000. Some complain that Hilo is too wet and is plagued by rot, mold, and various critters. Working and shopping there we have not found the almost daily showers to be oppressive.

Waikiki, Honolulu, island of Oahu A revitalized Waikiki area with its many apartments and condominiums could be just the ticket for the urbanized retiree. Waikiki area rehabilitation and revitalization plans come and go. The latest proposals would create walkways, bicycle lanes and a "beautification" of the Ala Wai Canal, along with elimination of the long popular Ala Wai public golf course. If you are looking for action, entertainment, nightlife, a date or a mate, opt for a short term rental and stay as long as your energy and money last.

Well, there they are to tempt and taunt you. You can agree, disagree, dismiss, debate or detour around any or all of the above. Our selections are meant to be tantalizing and revealing. But our "top ten," along with a map of each island and a will to retire in Hawaii, should set you to thinking and exploring. If you are as fortunate as we were, you will likely find just that place you fantasized about. If you find it, write us and tell us where, when, and above all <u>why</u> you chose what you did. If you don't, let us know where and how Hawaii failed to meet your expectations. In any event, we wish you a happy, healthy and prosperous retirement.

Epilogue: Whither Hawaii

Twenty-five years ago Alvin Toffler warned of the impending consequences of technological advances and accelerated rate of technological and social change in *Future Shock*.[clxvi] His proposed solution, as expressed in a clever piece of phraseology, is to be found in "anticipatory democracy," a broad based political system which anticipates change and marshals resources to cope with such change rather than suffer it. This massive and quickened pace of change has played itself out in Hawaii in economic development and environmental depletion that some residents of Hawaii regard as the twin plagues of Western or American invention.

Recently, Ken Dychtwald posted similar warnings re an impending "age wave." In *Age Power* (1999) Dychtwald analyzes the coming struggle for political power in the 21st century. His analysis focuses on the demographics of the aging process and the conflicts between needs, values, and resources that will tend to concentrate wealth, land, consumer demand and electoral clout in the hands of those over 60 years of age. His subtitle succinctly states the thesis: How the 21st century will be ruled by the new old. "America," Dychtwald contends, is becoming a "gerontocracy,"[clxvii] "In the year 2000, approximately 76 million Americans will be past the age of 50: This is exactly the number of Americans that there were—in total—in the year 1900. It's as though the American nation is giving birth to a "senior nation" and the 20th century was the gestation period."[clxviii]

Dychtwald's argument will be writ large in Hawaii partly because of the age dynamics of the current resident population resulting in smaller families, lower reproduction rates, and multigenerational families. The implicit conflict will be intensified by in-migration and the influx of retirees, semi-permanent visitors, second and vacation home dwellers, and hybrid residents who will be dependent on as well as contribute to the local economy. Not age alone, but age related wealth and power (or lack of it) will be the determinants of social policy, legislation, and actual practice. Adapting a well-worn phrase, those who can pay will call the tune in Hawaii as elsewhere. And, as elsewhere, Hawaii may not be prepared for the consequences.[clxix]

Could Hawaii become a gerontocracy with values, trends and institutions dominated by the silver and gold set? Under some scenarios this is not merely likely it is virtually certain. Will elders constitute a non-productive drain on society's resources? Declining productivity, and dwindling employment among seniors could lead to unmitigated dependence on social resources, but the resources those over 55 control and invest could be the capital that drives Hawaii's economy as the 21st century unfolds.

Hawaii has the highest life expectancy in the U.S. and the population is the third fastest aging population in the fifty states.[clxx] These trends will play a highly significant role throughout the early decades of he 21st century. What then are the implications of these demographic trends?

The effect could be more pronounced, more prolonged and more severe, a class struggle between young and old and between those who have and those who have not.

Is it possible that Hawaii could become the most "gerontified" state in the U.S. unique in the entire world? Many residents of Hawaii, especially those born and bred in the islands, are aware that the future is problematic and likely to be fraught with such controversy. This in part is due to Hawaii's inbred culture and insularity, which magnifies and focuses local trends and events through an odd historical prism. Local pride and prejudice reinforces itself as the future keeps bearing down in the form of the booms and busts, environmental stress, shortages and increasing cost of land, goods and services that, in spite of the glitz and apparent luxury, suppress Hawaii's overall standard of living. New waves of residents will intensify this problem, but they could lead to a resolution and amelioration by virtue of the new capital they infuse into the economy.

Dychtwald observes that, "...today's elders have grown in numbers, have become powerful and influential, and have managed to become more financially secure than any group in our nation's history. They are extraordinarily well connected, vote in higher concentrations than any other age group, and have AARP –the country's largest special interest group–to lobby for their interests."[clxxi] Their collective impact in Hawaii could be unparalleled and unprecedented in the 21st century.

In the decades to come, Hawaii will continue to be a major tourist destination. The lush tropical islands will bring solace and refuge for some, fulfillment and productive leisure for others. The 21st century will also bring thousands, perhaps tens of thousands, of full or part time residents. They will emerge in numbers that will have a double-edged impact on the islands and the economy of Hawaii. Presently, modest retirement in Hawaii is still possible. Although land prices have soared since 1960 and the boom of the 1970's there are good values in both land and housing because of over-development in some areas and the recent recession. However, housing stock is dwindling, new projects are slow and cumbersome, and list prices are beginning to move upward, especially on Oahu and Maui.

Retiring to Hawaii, even if only for vacation stints and retreats, requires interfacing one's future with that of Hawaii. So each prospective retiree must grapple with the questions regarding the future of Hawaii and the impact of incoming retirees on that future.

As we conclude, the answer to our seminal question – Is Hawaii friendly to retirees, seniors and elders who relocate there? –will carry us a long way in our assessment and appreciation of Hawaii as a retirement site.

The possible outcome of seemingly unfettered economic development geared to tourism and the incoming affluent retirees alongside a floundering local and native population is likely to generate a dual process of gentrification and ghettoization of the islands. It could lead to upscale retirement enclaves and local ghettos, neither integrated with the other but nonetheless shaping it in part and leading to further economic and social stratification. This could generate a parallel universe of rich and poor, one providing jobs for the other, one serving the other as a labor force. This trend is but an extension of the process of economic dualism that is inimical to both democracy and long-term improvements in the standard of living.[clxxii]

As new residents come to Hawaii the result will be dramatic and sweeping changes, incremental to be sure from 2000 to 2030, but over time again changing the face of Hawaii and its course through history as the immigrant, outsider or foreigner (*haole*) has done on several occasions in the past.

The next great influx is likely to be the capital-bearing elders and seniors drawn to Hawaii's healthy environment and pastoral lifestyle. They will need housing and transportation, food and entertainment, special services and medical care. And most of them will be able to pay for it, i.e. they will bring not only culture and their own lifestyle modifications, but capital and effective demand for all kinds of goods and services peculiar to the over-55 age group. They will likely have a greater impact in Hawaii than elsewhere, as they had impact and effect in St. Petersburg, Florida, Palm Springs, California and Scottsdale, Arizona. In those communities, the senior segment and older age groups tend to dominate the economy, politics and culture.

This gentrification/ghettoization process is a part of the economic dualism of rich and poor that characterizes much of Polynesia, Hawaii and other island regions, relics of colonialism, imperialism and expansionism.[clxxiii] The dual process of gentrification and ghettoization could produce a social stratification further displacing and dispossessing both groups, eventually forcing them into an uneasy alliance of master and servant. The disparity could become pronounced and further aggravated by the vicissitudes of the Native Hawaiian sovereignty and reconciliation movement, whereby the aboriginal indigenous population, the *Kanaka Maoli*, is pitted against the recent immigrant and transplant population.[clxxiv]

This leads us to pose yet other more specific questions that bear on Hawaii's future. Most of the previous efforts to prognosticate, predict and project Hawaii's future have focused on everything (environmental depletion, economic dislocation, military expenditures, intermarriage, etc.) except the impact of the aging population and the influx of retirees.[clxxv] Noteworthy exceptions are the Governor's 2030 Project, Project 2011 from the Office of Aging, and a 1999 report shepherded by urban planners Professor Karl Kim and Delores Foley, entitled *Babyboomers and Retirement: Challenges and Opportunities*. In a parallel study entitled Project 2011: a Strategic Plan for Action, Office of Aging, 1998. They contend that

"The "Boomer" cohort will significantly influence society and public policy...Hawaii, like the rest of the nation, is in the midst of a major demographic revolution...In the coming decades, the aging of our community will create unprecedented economic, political, and social challenges...Hawaii, which has a long history of welcoming new immigrants and diversity, has begun to show signs of strain. In addition, the significance of the Hawaiian Sovereignty movement both politically and economically needs to be recognized."[clxxvi]

So we again, at the close of our inquiry, pose the question that has guided our personal inquiry: is Hawaii retiree-friendly? The answer is still a qualified "yes." In spite of the price of paradise, in spite of importation of plastic culture alongside attempts to preserve timeworn traditional lifestyles (especially Hawaii's elegant rural simplicity) and in spite of the coming congestion and strain on the infrastructure and government services, Hawaii remains at the top of many lists detailing this or that senior Mecca or retirement Eden.[clxxvii] Hawaii is and will likely be a palette of colors from which one may compose life for at least another generation. Can Hawaii sustain a long-term future as an earthly paradise, or, as we have suggested, a playground for the affluent and leisure laden? Will Hawaii be retiree/senior-friendly a century from now? We leave that to you and others to ponder and to determine.

Tourism has struggled to remain the island economy's mainstay. It's difficult to live here and not be caught up in the issue: should we encourage more visitors? Will that entail more development and lead to more crowding? Will it really generate more money and jobs? Do the residents of Hawaii really want a populace that runs the gamut from island-born natives and third-and-fourth generation plantation workers to first-time investors, new retirees, and transplants from around the world?[clxxviii] These questions ring throughout the islands with many implications for both local and "foreign" retirees.

James R. Smith, Ph.D. Diane Smith, B.S.

Most Mainlanders are unaware of the significant momentum and potential impact of the Native Hawaiian Sovereignty movement on the future of Hawaii. In 1985 a constitution was fashioned by Native Hawaiians. In 1993 the so-called "apology law" was passed laying a moral and political foundation for recognition and reconciliation with the claims and demands of Native Hawaiians. In 2000, however, a Supreme Court decision checked this momentum by holding that Office of Hawaiian Affairs trustees may have been wrongfully elected and that non-Hawaiians could not be banned from voting for OHA trustees nor from holding such office in the future.[clxxix] Also in 2000 a bill was introduced by Senator Akaka (D-Hawaii) known as the Reconciliation Act calling for legislation intended to establish an independent nation for Native Hawaiians.[clxxx] (a "nation within a nation" as some would have it) The ultimate impact of these legislative mandates could disrupt the social fabric and ethnic harmony in Hawaii, and slow the growth of tourism, retard population increases and inhibit economic development. Prospective retirees, whatever their status and whatever their origin, should educate themselves regarding the movement and surrounding issues. It could affect the course of Hawaii's history and it could affect the quality of life throughout the Islands well into the 21st century.

At the extreme various factions pledge civil disobedience, social disruption, and concerted action if their demands are not accommodated. Some fringe elements threaten to secede from the United States, if they are successful; others threaten violence, if they are not.

The implications are disturbing and the impact could, in some quarters, signal the end of aloha, a shift from welcoming visitors to attempting to ban or limit them in spite of Statehood and the tenets of the U.S. Constitution.[clxxxi] In the worst case, it could make of Hawaii a closed or insular society of which Niihau is the contemporary prototype. The Haole Go Home sign is not visible just yet, but the sentiment is there in some quarters.[clxxxii]

If, and it's a big if, the Native Hawaiian secessionists and would be monarchists have their way, Hawaii could cease to be a desirable site for in-migrant retirees, a sad outcome of political upheaval and cultural transformation.

Despite the deeply imbedded "spirit of *aloha*" in the hybrid culture of Hawaii today, there are limits that any newcomer, retiree or visitor, are likely to encounter. Do not be seduced into thinking that *aloha* is universal. There are those, in places high and low, among all ethnic groups but most notably among Native Hawaiians themselves, who do not welcome you and who are distinctly averse to your presence, your money, and your Mainland lifestyle. For some, your very presence is an affront precisely because of your color and/or ethnic origin.

Much of this can be attributed to Hawaii's historic insularity. There is an "island" mentality characterized by a resistance to change, a preoccupation with the status quo and a measure of distrust for foreign influences and "imported" ideas. Would-be retirees are advised to be alert and aware of these cultural differences and their impact on the particular island or community one chooses for retirement.

Comments from long-time residents—both those born here and those who came years ago—include stories about the lack of acceptance and "outsider" status. It often takes up to ten years to feel accepted and thus a part of the community. The smaller islands (with smaller populations) of Kauai and Molokai have this reputation, especially when the newcomer is Euro-American.

Statehood opened the door for immigration which allowed all the rights and privileges of U.S. citizenship, a point lost in the tourism propaganda and rhetoric of the Native Hawaiian sovereignty movement. This controversy is important to retirees and lawful immigrants as it is likely to have a profound effect on their lives. Through this door have come new residents, new capital, fresh ideas and talents to mix into the population pool already in residence.

A major item retirees bring with them is their voting power.[clxxxiii] In future elections the silver set will be a strong force. The over-fifty-five group is likely to register to vote in increasing and disproportionate numbers as younger voters and citizens remain disenchanted. This is one of the American Association of Retired Person's (AARP) primary objectives: to organize older voters into an effective voting bloc and give expression to their priorities and needs.[clxxxiv] Statehood and citizenship have combined to create a political baseline for incoming residents, especially Euro-Americans from the Mainland.[clxxxv]

Statehood has encouraged and stimulated population growth and economic development. The U.S. Mainland will continue to be the primary source of new residents, including retirees and transplants. The local resident population is increased by local reproduction, but that increase could be offset by those migrating to the mainland for employment. If the Baby Boom numbers are at all accurate and persuasive, this continued influx could lead to a radical shift in Hawaii's ethnic composition, demographic configurations, and political landscape by the years 2020 through 2030.

The fallout from the vicious attacks of 9/11 was immediate and devastating in Hawaii as elsewhere. Tourism fell off sharply and real estate prices took a short-term tumble the local economy, like the rest of the united states and the world, is suffering. Reactions are mixed: some prognosticate that the movement to the rural islands that could be rapidly accelerated; others see Hawaii, especially Oahu, as quintessentially vulnerable. Whether it be mad bombers, eco-terrorists, nuclear attacks, or chemical/biological

agents, people in Hawaii are just as fearful of the terrifying potential for death and destruction as elsewhere. The world has again
shrunk and Hawaii will again be a paradise revised that is all too
accessible to benign tourists and miscreants alike.

Table 0-1 Suggested Reading and information sources

Useful information sources include the following:

1. *Reference Maps of the Islands of Hawaii*, James A. Bier, University of Hawaii Press. Maps of Hawaii, Kauai, Maui, Molokai-Lanai, and Oahu - full-color topographic with roads, parks, trails, and points of interest. A companion piece is the Atlas of Hawaii, also from University of Hawaii Press.
2. Gavan Daws, *Shoal of Time*, University of Hawaii Press, Honolulu 1974. Probably the most widely read account of the history of Hawaii. An excellent treatment of the history and development of Hawaii from native settlement to Capt. Cook's discovery in 1778 to Statehood. Also Cooper & Daws, *Land & Power* (University of Hawaii Press 1990)
3. Toni Polancy, *So You Want to Live in Hawaii*, a well written account of contemporary life in Hawaii.
4. *Hawaii Pono: A Social History* Lawrence H. Fuchs, Harcourt, Brace & World, Inc., New York 1961. A widely read treatment of the social and ethnic history of life in Hawaii.
5. Pacific Business News (weekly). A useful source for the business community. Many current statistics and issue oriented articles.
6. The State of Hawaii Public Library System - see Table 0-2- Library
7. Area Offices on Aging - Table 4-3
8. Newspapers-The Honolulu Advertiser and Star-Bulletin -see media list 1-3.
9. The State of Hawaii Data Book (annual comprehensive source, indispensable) 1998, A Statistical Abstract, DBEDT, The Department of Business Economic Development and Tourism, P. O. Box 2359, Honolulu 96804

10. Hawaii Data Book for Older Adults, Office on Aging
11. Department of Health and Human Services
Also worth consulting are statistics and data from
U. S. Department of Labor and U.S. Department of Interior
12. U. S. Department of Commerce (the parent agency for the U.S. Census), Census 2000 Series
   Two other sources are of great importance and should be consulted by anyone seriously considering relocating and retirement in Hawaii:
13. AARP (formerly the American Association of Retired Persons) publications, national and local - Newsletters, etc. - see Table 0-3, Hawaii AARP list.
14. The Smyser Report (1993)
15. Introductory pages of the GTE Hawaiian Tel phone books for each island and last, but certainly not least in either relevance or significance is the sovereignty/anti-sovereignty debate and collateral literature including two opposing points of view in The *Betrayal of Liliuokalani* by Helena G. Allen (Mutual Publishing 1982 and the trenchant response from Thurston Twigg-Smith entitled *Hawaiian Sovereignty: Do the Facts Matter?* (Goodale Publishing, Honolulu 1998)

   The two volume collection of monographs and editorial pieces, *The Price of Paradise*, (Roth, Randall W., Mutual Publishing, Honolulu 1992 and 1993) though now somewhat dated, are must reading for prospective retirees.

   Additional useful sources:

   Islands Under the Influence, Kent, Noel. A neo-Marxist perspective on the "discovery" of Hawaii by European and American business interests and the subsequent development of Hawaii as a military base and tourist destination.

   Islands in Transition, Hitch, Thomas Kemper, University of Hawaii Press 1992

Hi-Rise Hawaii, Krauss, Robert, Coward-McCann, Inc., New York 1969

Hawaii: The Legend that Sells, Farrell, Bryan, University of Hawaii Press, 1982

Guides to islands, e.g. beaches - travel literature, restaurant guides - helpful but not essential to the retirement minded. We enjoyed reading the following before and on our visits to various islands.

Hidden Hawaii, Ray Riegert, Ulysses Press, Berkeley, California 1999

Kauai Underground, Lenore W. Horowitz, Papaloa Press 1998

Hawaii, The Big Island Revealed, Andrew Doughty and Harriett Friedman, Wizard Publications 1999

This Week Visitor Magazine on each island - good maps and discount coupons for meals, gifts and film. Also on-line at www.thisweek.com.

The above sources and any others in this book are accurate to the best of our knowledge. Readers should bear in mind that phone numbers, e-mail and websites are subject to change.

Table 0-2 Library System

Hawaii State Public Library System is a valuable resource for visitors and future residents either in person or by internet - www.hcc.hawaii.edu/hspls/.

The system has branch libraries (several in schools) scattered on each island. The selection is good and librarians helpful. Special interest items may be ordered from other branches. Books are loaned for three weeks and can be renewed by phone. Videotapes are also available for $1.00 for loan period, which is 7 (seven) days. Hawaii residents receive a card at no cost. But a replacement card is $10.00. A non-resident card is $25.00 or a visitor's card (3-month) is $10.00. Many kupuna (elder, wise old person) are seen at libraries reading the daily newspapers, magazines, etc. They are up to date on a budget. The library system offers music, story-telling and other programs often and they are open to the public.

Table 0-3 AARP Hawaii Information Centers

Oahu AARP Information Center

1199 Dillingham Blvd., A-106, Honolulu 96817

808/843-1906, FAX 808/843-1908
Hawaii Information Center

P.O. Box 2078, Kailua-Kona 96745

808/334-1212, FAX 818/329-4894, email: hiknoa@aloha.net
Maui Information Center

562-A Front Street, Lahaina 96761

808/661-0159, FAX 808/667-7001, email: hilahain@maui.net
Kauai Information Center

4212-A Rice Street, Lihue 96766

808/246-4500, FAX 808/245-6172, e-mail: liaarp@aloha.ent

Table 1-1 Budget

Monthly Budget for Two People in Honolulu

Assumption 1

Utilities:	150
Car Insurance:	100
Gas/Repairs:	100
Health Insurance:	300
Food:	400
Miscellaneous:	100
Recreation/travel:	150
Property taxes:	100
Savings and misc.	<u>1,100</u>

$2500/month

$30,000/year

Assumption 1 - With this illustration, we assumed that the hypothetical couple has purchased a car or two and a home for cash. We also assume that they are not Medicare age - see health insurance.

Assumption 2 - low income

Rental apartment	400.00
Car	200.00
Food	400.00
Health Care	300.00
Savings and misc.	<u>150.00</u>

$1,450.00/month

Table 1-2 Real Property Tax Offices

Hawaii

Hilo - 865 Piilani St., 96720
808-961-8201

Kona - 75-5706 Kuakini Highway, Ste. 112
808-327-3540

Kauai

Lihue - 4444 Rice, Ste. 466
808-241-6555

Maui

Wailuku - 200 S. High
808-243-7705

Oahu

City and County of Honolulu
exemption/rates
842 Bethel
808-527-5510

elderly property tax relief program
530 S. King
808-523-4805

Table 1-3 Real Property Tax Rates by Counties: 2000

Tax rates per $1,000 net assessed value on land, building (improvements) and by property classification for Fiscal Year 2000 shown below.

Land use class	Honolulu	Maui	Hawaii	Kauai
Land:				
Improved Residential	3.65	5.04	8.50	
Unimproved residential	4.55	5.04	10.00	
Apartment	4.49	5.04	8.50	8.80
Hotel/resort	9.96	8.48	10.00	8.80
Commercial	9.25	6.89	10.00	8.80
Industrial:				
Agricultural	9.89	5.04	10.00	8.20
Conservation	9.25	5.04	10.00	8.20
Homeowner	0.00	3.71	4.45	0.00
Homestead	0.00	0.00	0.00	4.85
Building:				
Improved residential	3.65	5.04	8.50	0.00
Unimproved residential	4.66	5.04	8.50	0.00
Apartment	4.49	2.04	8.50	8.40
Hotel/resort	9.96	8.48	8.50	8.40
Commercial	9.25	6.89	8.50	4.75
Industrial				
Agricultural	9.89	6.89	8.50	4.75
Conservation	9.25	5.04	8.50	4.75
Homeowner	0.00	3.71	4.45	0.00
Homestead	0.0	0.00	0.00	3.99

Source: Tax Foundation of Hawaii -
http://www.tfhawaii.org/taxes/property.html

Assessments at 100% of "fair market value." In general, minimum exemption for owner-occupied homes is $40,000 with multiple exemptions based on age; specific exemption amounts may vary by county.

Table 1-4 Helpful Websites

Newspapers:
    Honolulu Advertiser: www.honoluluadvertiser.com
    Honolulu Star-Bulletin: www.starbulletin.com
    Maui News: www.mauinews.com
    West Hawaii Today (Kona):   www.westhawaiitoday.com
    Hawaii Tribune-Herald (Hilo): www.hilohawaiitribune.com
    Pacific Business News   www.amcity.com/pacific
News/Media:
                      www.interwave-hawaii.com/ListComm.html
                      www.enewshawaii.com

Hawaii Radio/TV Guide:
                      www.lava.net/~macpro/welcome.html

State of Hawaii - comprehensive site: www.state.hi.us
Hawaii State Public Library System: www.hcc.hawaii.edu/hspls/

Job Search
    Adecco   www.adecco-hawaii.com/
                      www.jobsearch.org/hi/
                      www.jobsurfhawaii.com

Other information   www.living-in-paradise.com

Institute for Rural Studies   **www.retire2hawaii.net**
Free Newsletter available

Table 1-5 Average Temperatures and Precipitation

Island	Elevation Feet	Coolest month	Warmest month	Rain inches
Hawaii:				
Hilo Airport	30	71.2	75.9	128
Volcanoes PK	970	57.6	63.2	101
Naalehu	800	70.2	75.1	47
Kailua-Kona	30	72.1	77.3	25
Mauna Kea	13796	31.3	42.5	20
Maui:				
Hana Airport	60	71.4	77.3	83
Haleakala	10025	42.6	50	44
Lahaina	45	71.5	78	15
Molokai:				
Molokai Airport	450	70.2	77.6	27
Oahu:				
Honolulu	10	72.6	81.0	23
Manoa	500	69.9	76.1	158
Kaneohe	200	71.0	77.5	71
Kauai:				
Kilauea	315	68.7	75.6	68
Lihue	100	71.3	77.5	44
Kekaha	9	71.0	78.5	21
Kokee	3600	54.7	63.8	70

Source: State of Hawaii Data Book 1999

Table 2-1 Population by Race for the State of Hawaii From 2000 Census

Total Population	Race Alone 1	Race Alone or in Combination2
Total Population	1,211,537	1,211,537
White	294,102	476,162
Black or African American	22,003	33,343
American Indian and Alaska Native	3,535	24,882
Asian	503,868	703,232
Native Hawaiian and Other Pacific Islander	113,539	282,667
Some other races	15,147	47,603

1   One of the following six races: (1) White, (2) Black or African American (3) American Indian and Alaska Native, (4) Asian, (5) Native Hawaiian and Other Pacific Islander, (6) Some other race

2   Alone or in combination with one or more of the other five races listed

Source: Hawaii Census 2000 www.hawaii.gov/dbedt/census2k

Table 2-2 Population Growth by Island

Island	1990	2000	% change
State of Hawaii	1,108,229	1,211,537	9.3
Oahu	836,231	876,156	4.8
Hawaii	120,317	148,677	23.6
Maui	91,361	117,644	28.8
Lanai	2,426	3,193	31.6
Molokai	6,717	7,404	10.2
Kauai	50,947	58,303	14.4
Niihau	230	160	30.4

Source: Hawaii Census 2000
www.hawaii.gov/dbedt/census2k

Table 4-1
Median Sales Price of Single Family and Condominium Resales 1989–1999

Single Family	State Total	% Change	Oahu	% Change	Hawaii	% Change	Kauai	% Change
1989	236,565		270,000		136000		204,000	
1990	287,617	22	355,000	31	150000	10	260,000	27
1991	286,026	(1)	345,000	(3)	165000	10	247,500	(5)
1992	281,220	(2)	349,000	1	154250	(7)	185,000	(25)
1993	292,359	4	350,000	0	170000	10	231,613	25
1994	295,982	1	360,000	3	165000	(3)	24,450	6
1995	280,932	(5)	349,000	(3)	155000	(6)	250,000	2
1996	274,918	(2)	344,000	(1)	165000	6	219,000	(12)
1997	253,675	(8)	305,000	(11)	155000	(6)	221,000	1
1998	251,500	(1)	297,000	(3)	159000	3	237,500	7
1999	253,000	1	290,000	(2)	165000	3	238,750	1

Condo	State Total	% Change	Oahu	% Change	Hawaii	% Change	Kauai	% Change
1989	236,565		270,000		136000		204,000	
1990	287,617	22	355,000	31	150000	10	260,000	27
1991	286,026	(1)	345,000	(3)	165000	10	247,500	(5)
1992	281,220	(2)	349,000	1	154250	(7)	185,000	(25)
1993	292,359	4	350,000	0	170000	10	231,613	25
1994	295,982	1	360,000	3	165000	(3)	24,450	6
1995	280,932	(5)	349,000	(3)	155000	(6)	250,000	2
1996	274,918	(2)	344,000	(1)	165000	6	219,000	(12)
1997	253,675	(8)	305,000	(11)	155000	(6)	221,000	1
1998	251,500	(1)	297,000	(3)	159000	3	237,500	7
1999	253,000	1	290,000	(2)	165000	3	238,750	1

State of Hawaii Data Book 1999 - Source: Data compiled by Prudential Locations Research

Table 4-2 SENIOR RESIDENCE FACILITIES

POHAI NANI GOOD SAMARITAN KAUHALE
45-090 Namoku Street, Kaneohe, Oahu
808/247-6211
www.assistguide.com/pohainani
208 residential units, 42 SNF/ICF beds

THE PONDS AT PUNALU'U
53-594 Kamehameha Highway, Hauula, Oahu
808/293-1100
www.assistguide.com/theponds

THE ARCADIA RETIREMENT RESIDENCE
1434 Punahou Street, Honolulu, Oahu
808/941-0941
www.arcadia-hi.org

HOLIDAY RETIREMENT CORPORATION
c/o HKRC
428 Kawaihae Street, Honolulu, Oahu 96825
808/395-9599
Neighbor Islands/mainland 1-800-324-1295
Hawaii Kai on Oahu is HRC's first facility.
Other accommodations will soon be available on Maui.

REGENCY AT HUALALAI
75-181 Hualalai Road, Kailua-Kona, Big Island
808/329-7878
www.RetirementHawaii.com
e-mail: carole@retirementhawaii.com
129 apartments – includes Alzheimer's unit.

VILLA VITAL, "Home-Away-From-Home" Assisted Living
P. O. Box 1715, Kailua, Oahu 96734
808/551-1405
Email: villavital@hawaii.rr.com

A partial list can also be found at www.assistguide.com

Table 4-3 Area Agencies on Aging

Big Island

Hilo	808/961-8600
Kona	808/327-3597

Maui

Maui County Office on aging	808/270-7755
FAX	808/270-7935
Kauai	808/245-1100
Oahu	808/586-0100
Elderly Information and Assistance Services	808/523-4545
Long Term Care Ombudsman	808/586-0100
FAX	808/586-0185

Table 5-1 Hospitals in Hawaii by Island

Big Island
Hilo Medical Center:	808/974-4700
Honokaa Hospital:	808/775-7211
Kau Hospital:	808/928-8331
Kohala Hospital:	808/889-6211
Kona Community Hospital:	808/322-9311
North Hawaii Community Hospital:	808/885-4444

Maui
Kula Hospital:	808/878-1221
Maui Memorial Medical Center:	808/244-9056

Kauai
West Kauai Medical Center:	808/338-9531
St. Francis Medical Center:	808/245-2972
Wilcox Memorial Center:	808/245-1100

Oahu
Castle Medical Center	808/263-5500
Kahuku Hospital	808/293-9221
Kuakini Medical Center	808/536-2236
Kaiser Foundation Hospital	808/834-5333
Kapiolani Medical Center	808/486-6000
The Queen's Medical Center	808/538-9011
St. Francis Medical Center	808/547-6011
St. Francis Medical Center, West	808/678-7000

James R. Smith, Ph.D. Diane Smith, B.S.

Straub Clinic and Hospital   808/522-4000
Wahiawa General Hospital   808/621-8411

Table 5-2 Hawaii Health Plans

HMSA (Blue Cross/Blue Shield affiliate)
www.hmsa.org
670 Ponahawai Street, Suite 121
Hilo, HI, 96720
808/935-5441 (Hilo) 808/329-5291 (Kona)
Locations: Oahu, Big Island, Kauai, Maui

Kaiser Permanente Medical Care Program
www.kaiserpermanente.org
Hualalai Medical Center
75-184 Hualalai Road
Kailua-Kona, HI, 96740
809/327-2929 (Kona)
Locations: Oahu, Big Island, Kauai, Maui

The Queen's Health Plans
www.queens.org
P.O. Box 60
Honolulu, HI, 96808
1-800-651-4672
Locations: Oahu, Big Island, Kauai, Maui, Molokai

Kapiolani HEALTHHAWAII
www.kapiolani.org
55 Merchant Street
Honolulu, HI, 96813
1-800-352-4572
Locations: Oahu, Big Island, Kauai, Maui, Molokai

James R. Smith, Ph.D. Diane Smith, B.S.

Queen's Island Care
75 Puuhonu Place, Suite 206
Hilo, HI, 96720
808/961-5771

HMMA
1585 Kapiolani Blvd., Suite 900
Honolulu, HI, 96814
1-800-621-6998
Locations: Oahu, Big Island, Kauai, Maui

Table 5-3 Hospice Services in Hawaii

Big Island
      Hospice of Hilo
      1011 Waianuenue Avenue, Hilo 96720
      808/969-1733

Hospice of Kona

      P.O. Box 217, Kailua-Kona 96740
      808/334-0334

North Hawaii Hospice

      P.O. Box 1236, Kamuela 96743
      808/885-7547

Kauai
      Kauai Hospice, Lihue 96766
      808/245-7277

Maui
      Hospice Maui
      400 Mahalani Street, Wailuku 96793
      808/244-5555

Oahu
      Hospice Hawaii
      860 Iwilei Road, Honolulu 96817
      808/924-9255

      Respite Care of Hawaii, Inc.
      566 Papalani, Kailua 967347
      808/262-4055

      Sister Maureen Keleher Center
      24 Puiwa Road, Honolulu 96817
      808/595-7566

Table 7-1 Cookbooks

A Taste of Hawaii, New Cooking from the crossroads of the Pacific,
Jean-Marie Josselin, Coco Masuda, Tabori & Change, Inc. 2000

Eating Well in Hawaii: Fish and Poi Chefs' Low-Fat Recipes,
Patricia Salvador, Joannie Dobbs, Alfred Salvador, Jr., Mutual
Publishing Company 1998

Ethnic Foods of Hawaii, Ann Condo Corum, The Bess Press, Inc.
2000

Flavors of Hawaii: Recipes Celebrating Hawaii's Diversity, Wimer,
Al Furtado, Child & family Enterprises, Inc. 1998

Hawai's BEST Cookbook on Fried Rice, Yoshida, George, Big Island
Printers, Hilo, HI.

Hawaii Cooking with Aloha, Elvira Monroe, Irish Margah, Wide
World Publishing/Tetra 1995

Hawaii's Island Cooking, Bonni Tuell, Mutual Publishing
Company 1996

Hawaii's Spam Cookbook, Ann Condo Corum, The Bess Press
1995

Roy's Feasts from Hawaii: A Culinary Tour of the Hawaiian Islands,
Roy Ramaguchi with John Harrison, Ten Speed Press 1994

Sam Choy's Island Flavors: Cook your Way to Paradise with More than 200 Delicious Recipes from Hawaii's Master Chef, Sam Choy, Hyperion 1999

The Food of Paradise: Exploring Hawaii's Culinary Heritage, Rachel Laudan, University of Hawaii Press 1996

Vegetarian Nights: Fresh From Hawaii, Bonnie Mandoe, Ten Speed Press 1994

Hawaiian Terms

Aloha - Hello, goodbye, love

Grinds - food

Hapa- half; person of mixed blood

Haole - foreigner, especially Caucasian

Hula - traditional Hawaiian dance

Halau - hula school, performance group

Kamaaina - Hawaiian resident, local person. Airlines and hotels give discounts to residents called "kamaaina rates."

Kane - man - used on bathroom doors

Kapu - taboo, forbidden

Kapuna - elder, wise one

Keiki - child, children

Kine - that thing, anything being referred to, also: that kind of thing

Kokua - caring, giving of self, polite - seen at video store - please kokua; please rewind

Kupuna – grandparent, ancestor or friend of grandparent's generation

Lanai – porch, veranda

Lua - bathroom

Luau - feast

Mahi-mahi - a popular fish, a form of dolphin

Mahalo - thank you

Makai – ocean; toward the ocean

Malasada – Portuguese donut without a hole

Mauka – mountain; toward the mountain

Ohana - family; also an additional dwelling on a property

Ono - name of a fish; also good or delicious (ono grinds = good food)

Pakalolo – marijuana

Paniolo - Hawaiian cowboy

Pau - finished, all gone, end

Pau hana - end of work (commute time is referred to as pau hana time.)

Pono - right action

Puka - hole, puka shells (hole), opening, door

Pupu – appetizer, snack

Talk story - make small talk, gossip or bargain - e. g., Want $100 for car, but will talk story.

Wahine - woman, female - wahine basketball, volleyball and other wahine sports are assiduously followed by local residents. Commonly posted on bathroom doors.

Bibliography

Abbey, Lana, *Moving to Hawaii, A Comprehensive Guide to Moving to Oahu*, Paradise Valley Publications Las Vegas, Nevada, 1995

Adler, Peter S., *Beyond Paradise*, Ox Bow Press, Connecticut 1993

Allen, Helena G., *The Betrayal of Liliuokalani*, Mutual Publishing, Honolulu 1982

Benhamn, Yalanda J., *How to Live in Hawai on $1000 per Month*, Roco Press,Kona, Hawaii 1994

Bornhorst, Heidi, "Hawaii Gardens," Honolulu Advertiser, 26 December 1999

Bratton, Joseph, *How to Retire in Hawaii on a Lot Less Than You'd Think*, Pau Hana Pres, Honolulu 1983

Budnick, Rich, *Stolen Kingdom, An American Conspiracy*, Aloha Press, 1992

Carter, Frances, *Hawaii for Free, Hundreds of Free Things to do in Hawaii*, Mustang Publishing, Memphis, TN. 194

Chaplin, George and Glenn D. Paige, *Hawaii 2000*, University Press of Hawaii 1973

Cieply, Michael, "East of Eden," Forbes, Inc. January 1983

Clark, John R.K., *Beaches of the Big Island*, University of Hawaii Press 1993

Clarke, Joan, *Local Food, What to Eat in Hawaii*, Namkoong Pubishing, Honolulu
1997

Cole, Elizabeth and Jonathan, *Move To Hawaii, Information on Relocation to the Island of Hawaii*, Hawaii Settlers Bureau, 1989

Cooper, George, and Gavan Daws, *Land Power in Hawaii*, University of Hawaii Press, Honolulu 1990

Corum, Ann Kondo, *Ethnic Foods of Hawaii*, The Bess Press, Inc. 2000

Daws, Gavan, *Shoal of Time: A History of the Hawaiian Islands*, University of Hawaii Press, Honolulu 1974

Dickinson, Peter A., *Retirement Edens*, American Asociation for Retired Persons, 1987

Donohugh, Don, and Bea, *Kauai: A Paradise Guide*, Paradise Publications, 1987

Doughty, Andrew, and Harriett Friedman, *Hawaii: The Big Island Revealed*, Wizard Publications 1999

Dychtwald, Ken, *AgePower*, Tarcher/Putnam, 1999

Farrrell, Bryan H., *Hawaii: The Legend that Sells*, University of Hawaii Press, 1982

Filipino Women's League, *Hawaii Filipinas' Favorite Recipes*, Filipino Women's League, Pearl City, Hawaii, 1999

Fuchs, Lawrence H., *Hawaii Pono: A Social History*, Harcourt, Brace & World, Inc., New York 1961

Hammel, Faye and Sylvan Levey, *Frommer's Budget Travel Guide, Hawaii '95 on $75 a Day*, Macmillan Travel, N.Y. 1995

Hitch, Thomas Kamper, *Islands in Transition*, University of Hawaii Press 1992

Kame'eleihiwa, Lilikala, *Native Land and Foreign Desires*, Bishop Museum Press, Honolulu 1992

Kent, Noel J., *Hawaii: Islands Under the Influence*, University of Hawaii Press, Honolulu 1993

Kodani, Roy M., *Open House, a Guide to Buying and Selling Hawaii Real Estate*, University of Hawaii Press 1996

Chaplin, George and Glenn F. Page, *Hawaii 2000*, Continuing Experiment in Anticipatory Democracy, University of Hawaii Press 1973

Krauss, Bob, *High-Rise Hawaii*, Coward-McCann, Inc., New York 1969

McDermott, John and Bobbye Hughes, *Zagat Survey*, 1998 Hawaii Restaurants, Zagat Survey, LLC 1998

Mandoe, Bonnie, *Vegetarian Nights, Fresh from Hawaii*, Celestial Arts, Berkeley, CA. 1994

Margan, Joseph R., *Hawaii: A Unique Geography*, The Bess Press, Honolulu 1996

Myatt, Carl, *The Insider's Guide to Hawaii*, Hunter Publishing, Inc., Edison, N.J. 1993

Napier, A. Kam, "The Writing on the Wall," Honolulu Magazine, September 1998

Ochwat, Tom, *Hawaii Real Estate - Investment Guide*, Hawaiian International Trade Publications, 1980

Oliver, Anthony Michael, *Hawaii Fact and Reference Book*, Mutual Publishing, Honolulu 1995

Paxman, David, *A Newcomer's Guide to Hawaii*, Mutual Publishing, Honolulu 1993

Penisten, John, Hawaii, *The Big Island, Making the Most of Your Family Vacation*, Paradise Publications, 1999

Pietsch, James H. and Lenora H. Lee, *The Elder Law Hawaii Handbook*, University of Hawaii Press 1998

Polancy, Toni, *So You Want to Live in Hawaii*, Barefoot Publishing, Honolulu 1998

Pukui, Mary Kawena and Samuel H. Elbert, *New Pocket Hawaiian Dictionary*, University of Hawaii Press, Honolulu 1992

Ravel, Sally and Lee Ann Wolfe, *Retirement Living*, Conari Press, Berkeley 1990

Riegert, Ray, *Hidden Hawaii*, Ulysses Press, Berkeley, California 1999

Roth, Randall W., *The Price of Paradise*, Mutual Publishing, Honolulu 1992

Roth, Randall W., *The Price of Paradise Vol. II*, Mutual Publishing, Honolulu 1993

Smith, Zachary A. and Richard C. Pratt, *Politics and Public Policy in Hawaii*, State University of New York Press, Albany, 1992

Staples, Gerge W. and Michael S. Kristiansen, *Ethnic Culinary Herbs, A Guide to Identification and Cultivation in Hawaii*, State University of New York Press, Albany, 1992

Twigg-Smith, Thurston, *Hawaiian Sovereignty: Do the Facts Matter?*, Goodale Publishing, Honolulu 1998

Weaver, Peter, *How to Stretch Your Retirement Dollar*, Information Videos, Silver Spring, MD. 1993

Whittaker, Elvi, *The Mainland HAOLE, The White Experience in Hawaii*, Columbia University Press 1986

Yoshida, George, *Hawai's BEST Cookbook on Fried Rice*, Big Island Printers, Hilo, HI.

ⁱ Bratton, Joseph, *How to Retire in Hawaii on a Lot Less Than You'd Think*, Pau Hana Press, Honolulu 1983 – and most books were tour guides or guides to hiking trails or hidden beaches etc. One was merely an "assist" to relocation.

ⁱⁱ Smith and Smith, *Life on the Island of Orchids and Ohia Trees*, 2001

ⁱⁱⁱ *Oxford Universal Dictionary*, Third Edition, 1952, p. 1428. See also paradise defined as an earthly state, i.e. an Eden. See also Daws, Gavan, *A Dream of Islands*, p. 19. "The idea of some sort of earthly paradise in the South Seas in fact lived on into the nineteenth century. It was by its nature inextinguishable, irrepressible."

^{iv} The theory of ludenics has found application in explaining a wide range of human behaviors, including the learning process, the creative process and sexual behaviors. Its value in medical science in pediatrics, psychiatry and psychopathology is well documented. 'Adult play is defined as spontaneous, free-flowing, creative, joyous, or pleasurable activity. Relatively devoid of structure and without the element of competition, it is essentially a leisure activity with directions emerging from within the person. . ." Otto and Otto, Total Sex, p. 299, italics in original. See also Huizinga, *Homo Ludens, a Study of the Play Elements in Culture*, Boston, Beacon, and Thorstein Veblen, Theory of the Leisure Class (1899).

^v Basically, the theory contends that the end (or fulfillment) of life is play, creative, undirected, spontaneous, even frivolous activity directed to no specific goal. See also Huizinga, *Homo Ludens, a Study of the Play Elements in Culture*, Boston, Beacon, and Thorstein Veblen, *Theory of the Leisure Class* (1899).

[vi] ludenics – may be characterized as a field of inquiry parallel to the Greek hedonics, the principles or dynamics of, or the ethical analysis of, hedonism, i.e., the pursuit of pleasure as the proper end of life or test of rightness. Hedonics is, briefly, the study of the pleasure principle, while ludenics is the study or philosophy of play.

[vii] Hitch, Thomas Kemper, *Islands in Transition*, University of Hawaii Press, 1992

[viii] Writing in Small Business News, September 2001

[ix] Dickinson, Peter A. *Retirement Edens: Outside the Sunbelt*, American Association of Retired Persons, Glenview Illinois, 1987 p. 1

[x] Ravel, Sally and Lee Ann Wolfe, *Retirement Living*, Conari Press, Berkeley 1990

[xi] Bratton, Joseph, *How To Retire In Hawaii On a Lot Less Than You'd Think*, Pau Hana Press, Honolulu, 1983

[xii] Weaver, Pete and John Spiropaulos, *How To Stretch Your Retirement Dollar*, Information Videos, Silver Spring, MD, 1993

[xiii] Farrell, Bryan, *Hawaii: The Legend That Sells*, University of Hawaii Press, 1982 p. 252. See also *Price of Paradise Vol. One*, p. 23.

[xiv] Adler, Peter S., et al., "Paradise Tax," *Price of Paradise*, Mutual Publishing, Honolulu 1993 p. 117

[xv] Mason, George, "Cost of Living Differential Not Really All That Bad," *Pacific Business News*, November 22, 1999

[xvi] Benham, Yolanda J., *How to Live in Hawaii on $1000.00 per Month*, Rico Press, Kona, Hawaii 1994, p. 20

[xvii] *The Honolulu Advertiser* website is www.honoluluadvertiser.com, and the *Honolulu Star Bulletin* is www.starbulletin.com. Other helpful listings are found in Table 1-3.

[xviii] Foley, T. M., "Property Tax Fairness," *Price of Paradise Vol. One*, Mutual Publishing, Honolulu 1992 p. 126

[xix] Suyderhoud, Jack, "Business Taxes," *Price of Paradise*, (Mutual Publishing, Honolulu 1992) page 133

xx Moving expenses may be tax-deductible expenses if you are moving to a new job or business. Consult your tax advisor.

xxi Morgan, Joseph, *Hawaii: a Unique Geography*, The Bess Press, Honolulu, 1996, p.1

xxii Polancy, Toni, *So You Want to Live in Hawaii*, Barefoot Publishing, Honolulu 1998

xxiii See Morgan, Joseph, *Hawaii: a Unique Geography*, "Urbanization" by Jon Goss and Matthew McGranahagn, especially the discussion on the tourism-land development economy; 1945-1993. pp. 152-159. For an opposing point of view on this issue see *Price of Paradise Vol. II*, "Land Regulation," Kent Kieth, President Chaminade University, "Is Hawaii being over developed?" pp. 133-137. Keith observes that "Actually, we have plenty of land (4.1 million acres total) and most of it is open space. His conclusion is that "there is enough land in Hawaii for development," a generalization that bears scrutiny with the lessons of the past decade.

xxiv *Kamaaina* is a Hawaiian term meaning native born, but when it comes to discount rates, it usually means "local" and only requires a Hawaii driver's license or proof of residence.

xxv Morgan, Joseph R, *Hawaii: A Unique Geography*, The Bess Press, Honolulu 1996

xxvi Ibid. See also, Department of Geography, University of Hawaii, *Atlas of Hawaii*, 2nd ed. UH Press, 1983; Blumenstock and Price, *Climates of the U.S.*; and Gordon, Hawaii, *Climatography of the U.S.*, no. 60-51, Washington D.C., Department of Commerce, 1967

xxvii Laupahoehoe High School, *April Fools*, See Tsunami Museum in Hilo – website *www.tsunami.org.*

xxviii Pacific Business Index, Bank of Hawaii report: "Hawaii's economic recovery has turned into an expansion," *Pacific Business News*, February 11, 2000, pg. 7

xxix "West Hawaii in Feeding frenzy," *Hawaii Realtor Journal* (HRJ), April 2000, Stathie John Prattas, PB, Coast Properties, Ltd. See also HRJ, June 1999.

An article in the *Pacific Business News* also reported that sales were up in North Kona, South Kona, Kauai, and Oahu. "Kona go boom," Lyn Danninger, *Pacific Business News* 2/18/2000. See also, *The Honolulu Advertiser* article "Lavish homes lift economy" by Glenn Scott, November, 2000.

xxx *Pacific Business News*, 2/11/2000.

xxxi Polancy, Toni, *So You Want to Live in Hawaii*, Barefoot Publishing, Honolulu, 1998, p. 121

xxxii Ibid, pp. 112-138

xxxiii Crane, J.L. and M. Okinaka, "Social Dynamics of the Aloha State," *Politics and Public Policy*, State University of New York Press, Albany, 1992 p. 53

xxxiv See, e.g., J.L. Crane and A.M. Okinaka, "Social Dynamics of the Aloha State: The Population of Hawaii." And Dan Boylen, "Blood Runs Thick: Ethnicity as a factor in Hawaii's Politics" in Z.A. Smith and R.C. Pratt, *Politics and Public Policy in Hawaii*, 1992, State University of New York Press, Albany. See M.K. Dudley and K.K. Agard, *A Call for Hawaiian Sovereignty*, Na Kane O Ka Malo Press, 1990 and K. Dychtwald, *Age Wave* and *Age Power*.

xxxv The U.S. Census reports the total number of Hawaiians in the U.S. at 211,000, with 138,000 residing in the Islands, and an additional 72,000 people of Hawaiian ancestry living on the mainland U.S. Source: *The State of Hawaii Data Book 1998*, Table 1.31, p. 45.

xxxvi "*Haole*," pronounced "howlie," is a Hawaiian term, which means, foreigner or "white person." See *New Pocket Hawaiian Dictionary*, Mary Kawena Pukui and Samuel H. Elbert, University of Hawaii Press, 1997.

xxxvii For a balanced view of the sovereignty movement debate and collateral literature, see *The Betrayal of Liliuokalani,* by Helena G. Allen, Mutual Publishing, 1982 and the trenchant response from Thurston Twigg-Smith entitled *Hawaiian Sovereignty: Do the Facts Matter?* Goodale Publishing, Honolulu 1998

xxxviii Fuchs, Lawrence H., *Hawaii Pono: A Social History,* page vii (Harcourt, Brace and World, Inc., New York, 1961)

xxxix half, person of mixed blood

xl Odo, Franklin and Susan Smith, *The Price of Paradise,* Volume II, Mutual Publishing, Honolulu 1993, p. 227

xli *Ibid.* p. 229

xlii Boylan, Dan, "Blood Runs Thick: Ethnicity as a Factor in Hawaii's Politics," *Politics and Public Policy,* State University of New York Press, Albany, 1992 p. 69

xliii *Ibid.*

xliv For a sage treatment of the ethnic history of the islands see Gavan Daws' *Shoal of Time: A History of the Hawaiian Islands,* University of Hawaii Press, 1974

xlv See, e.g., the Insider-Outsider issue/debate in Hawaii Tribune Herald. Ultimately it turns on a question of relative acceptance and relative (or interactive) assimilation. See also Hitch, Thomas Kemper, *Islands in Transition,* University of Hawaii Press 1992.

xlvi For information about the Rice vs Cayetano lawsuit revolving around a long time non Hawaiian resident serving on or voting for the board of the Office of Hawaiian Affairs (OHA), see coverage in *The Honolulu Advertiser* – 1999 – 2000.

xlvii See, for example, the vociferous rhetoric from the lips of local *vox populi* Haunani Kay Trask, Office of Hawaiian Affairs trustee-at-large, who makes no bones about opposing the presence and presumed power of "the *Haole*" and "the Americans." Trask, Haunani Kay, First Friday, December 3, 1999 and elsewhere. See also "Kupaa Aina: Native Hawaii Nationalism in Hawaii," Haunani Kay Trask in *Politics and Public Policy*, pp. 243-260.

xlviii Crane, J.L. and M. Okinaka, "Social Dynamics of the Aloha State," *Politics and Public Policy*, (State University of New York Press, Albany, 1992) p. 54

xlix *Hawaii Summit: Project 2011*, Executive Office on Aging, 1998 p. 4

l DBEDT 2020 Series Projections, May 1997, p. 2

li *Ibid.*

lii Adler, Peter, et al., *Price of Paradise*, Mutual Publishing, Honolulu 1993.

liii Sources disagree as to the exact percentage of Caucasians and "mixed" whites in the general population. No one is sure exactly how much "white blood" is necessary to determine a person's race.

liv Goemans, John, *The Honolulu Advertiser*, Focus, February 2, 2000. (Attorney for Harold "Freddy" Rice in his lawsuit against the Hawaiians-only voting requirement for the Office of Hawaiian Affairs)

"Hawaiians were, by far, the largest voting bloc during the first 50 years of territorial government..."

lv See AARP Bulletin, February 2000, p. 3 "The battle to win the ballots of older voters...is shaping up to be more intense than ever this year." What is true on the national scale will be even more pronounced as Hawaii's population ages faster and lives longer than the U.S. average.

lvi AARP Policy Manual, Chapter One. See also legislative agenda for 1999 – 2000.

lvii Also see Chapter Five for a discussion of euthanasia, death with dignity and Hawaii as a hospice site.

lviii United States Census 2000, www.census.gov

"The number of Hawaii residents age 85 and older surged 69 percent, compared with a national average increase of 38 percent". Further statistics of interest include a 61 percent increase in the 75-84 year old population and a 57 percent increase in the 45-54 year old population". Christensen, Jean, Associated Press, "Census highlights a graying Hawaii," Hawaii Tribune Herald, May 18, 2001

lix Hawaii Tribune Herald, "Big Island is Most Diverse," 4/2000

lx See our comments: Chapter 3, Lanai

lxi Babbie, Earl, "The Maximillion Report," as cited in *The Price of Paradise*, Randall W. Roth, Mutual Publishing 1992.

lxii For further elaboration and documentation of this perspective see *Life on the Island of Orchids and Ohia Trees*, Smith and Smith, 2001.

lxiii Cooper, George, and Gavan Daws, *Land and Power in Hawaii*, University of Hawaii Press, Honolulu 1990

lxiv Every Beach on Oahu tends to be crowded. There are exceptions. On a 1996 research trip, we sought out sparsely populated beaches on Oahu's windward shores. Even on a weekday every beach was mobbed except Mokuleia Beach Park, near the north-west tip of Oahu (Kaena Point) where we found the solace and privacy we were seeking.

lxv *The Honolulu Advertiser*, January 30, 2000, p.1. See also "It's a Mess and There's No Way out," January 9, 2000, *The Honolulu Advertiser*. Also Rose, Louis A., "Traffic Congestion" in *The Price of Paradise Vol. II*, Mutual Publishing, 1993 pp. 151-157

lxvi Morgan, Joseph, *Hawaii: A Unique Geography*, The Bess Press 1996, p. 147

lxvii U. S. Census

lxviii Morgan, Joseph, *Hawaii: A Unique Geography*, The Bess Press 1996, p. 137

lxix Ibid. See also *Living in Waikiki*, a report on interviews with 48 Waikiki residents, The Planning Department, City and County of Honolulu, Dinell, Tom, assisted by Karl Kim, Professor of Urban and Regional Planning, University of Hawaii 1997. See also "Restoring Hawaiianness to Waikiki," George S. Kanahele, The Queen Emma Foundation 1994

2. Waikiki Master Plan, 1992 Department of General Planning, City and County of Honolulu and *The Price of Paradise* where several proposals were made to limit population on Oahu.

lxx *Aging in Hawaii: An Environmental Scan*, State of Hawaii, Executive Office on Aging, April 1992

lxxi See *101 Things to Do* on each island as well as other abundant tourist literature.

lxxii Office of the Chancellor, News Release 9/12/2000

lxxiii Ewa Beach scandal, etc., and various scams dating back to the 1950s; and the Really Big Scam (as seen through the eyes of the Hawaiian Native Society Movement, or the Great Land Grab of 1897, the result of a process of dispossession via protracted adverse possession).

lxxiv *Hawaii Real Estate Indicators: A Quarterly Report on the Real Estate Industry*, published by Prudential Locations in Honolulu. "Of particular note are the neighbor islands where [single family residential] resale activity thus far in 2000 is running at the highest annual rate ever."

lxxv *Ibid.*

lxxvi *Ibid.*

lxxvii *Ibid.* "Of particular note are the Waikiki condominiums where...prices are bouncing off levels last seen in the early 1980s."

lxxviii *Ibid.*

lxxix *The Price of Paradise*, p. 175, see also *Hawaii: A Unique Geography*, Morgan, Joseph R., p. 57

lxxx For more information and details on water availability and quality contact:

Oahu/Honolulu Board of Water Supply, 630 S. Beretania
Phone numbers: Information- 808/527-6124, Community Relations – 808/527-6126 See also Oahu Water Management Plan, Board of Water Supply, Honolulu July, 1982, and Oahu Water Management Plan, revised 1998.

For information on statewide and local rainfall and drought conditions contact:

1. Coast Guard, 800/426-9000
    www.uscg.mil/d14
2. www.epa/gov/region9
3. Recorded forecasts Honolulu 808/973-4380
    Surf – 808/973-4383
4. Tsunami Warning Center, Pacific 808/689-8207

[lxxxi] See the Editorial section of the *Honolulu Star-Bulletin* on November 28, 1999 regarding the sorry saga of Haunama Bay, where, old timers will tell you, Boy Scouts were once allowed to camp, thousands learned to snorkel and sea life and human use were once compatible.

[lxxxii] Polancy, Toni, *So You Want To Live in Hawaii*, Barefoot Publishing, 1998, p. 219

[lxxxiii] Sugar plantations provided the major source of employment on the Big Island until the final closings in 1996.

[lxxxiv] *Paniolo* is a Hawaiian-style cowboy. King Kamehameha III brought Spanish-Mexican vaqueros to Hawaii to work the ranches in 1832. *Paniolo* was adapted from the Spanish word to describe cowboys. *Paniolo* still ride the range in cattle country around Waimea.

[lxxxv] See Smith & Smith, *Retirees in Paradise*

lxxxvi Other than Lohii, the island forming beneath the waves sixty miles southeast of Hilo. It is not expected to break the surface for another 500,000 years.

lxxxvii Cannon-Eger, K.T., "Buyers: Big Island Ready for Mainland Buying Wave," *Hawaii Tribune-Herald*, May 16, 1999.

lxxxviii Ceil Sinnex, p 1.

lxxxix *Aging in Hawaii: An Environmental Scan*, State of Hawaii, Executive Office on Aging, April 1992

xc Waimea was voted one of 10 most desirable sites to live in the United States. See Fruits of our Labors, See also Smith and Smith, *Retirees in Paradise*.

xci mountain, toward the mountain

xcii The road to Hana is being repaired as of February 2000, which is bringing traffic distress to Maui residents and tourists.

xciii *Aging in Hawaii: An Environmental Scan*, State of Hawaii, Executive Office on Aging, April 1992

xciv Thomas, Sandy, "Kauai: Sigh of Relief as Market Turns Around on Garden Isle," *Pacific Business News*, June 4, 1999.

Thanks also to Phyllis Hamilton of Sleeping Giant Realty who told us about Sun Village condominiums, a retirement community located near Wilcox Memorial Hospital, WalMart and the Kauai bus express line. For further information, Contact Phyllis at 1-800-247-8831

xcv Molokai Drive Guide, April - September 1999. See also Smyser, A.A., *Hawaii's Future in the Pacific, Disaster, Backwater or Future State?*, The East-West Center, 1988

xcvi We were drawn to Molokai as early as 1969 and experienced its enchanting face of nature in a day long hike up the Halawa Valley at the island's lush easternmost shore.

xcvii Aloha, Hawaiian and Island Air offer monthly passes between $999 and $1099. Visitors can buy a seven-day pass for $321. *"Kamaaina"* rates are between $51 and $63 one-way inter-island.

xcviii "It remains to be seen how the island will develop in the future." Morgan, Joseph, *Hawaii: A Unique Geography*, The Bess Press, Honolulu 1996 p. 139.

xcix Cho, Frank, "Massive investment planned for Lanai," *The Honolulu Advertiser*, November 19, 2000. "Ever since, Lanai has been growing into a vacation fantasy for some of the worlds most rich and famous."

c Bricking, Tanya, *The Honolulu Advertiser*, "Lanai a kingdom on edge." July 2, 2000,

ci Bricking, Tanya, *The Honolulu Advertiser*, "Can Small Farms Succeed on Lanai?" February 20, 2000. For more information on this program contact Paul Matsuo of the State Department of Agriculture.

cii "Now that David Murdock chief executive of the privately held Castle & Cooke Inc. has undisputed control of nearly all of Lanai, he is preparing a wave of investment that could once again reshape the small island's fragile landscape."
Cho, Frank, "Massive investment planned for Lanai," *The Honolulu Advertiser*, November 19, 2000.
"Ever since, Lanai has been growing into a vacation fantasy for some of the worlds most rich and famous."
Ibid

ciii Morgan, Joseph, *Hawaii: A Unique Geography*, The Bess Press, Honolulu 1996

civ Ibid

cv Pacific Business News, June 1999

cvi Recent articles indicate a dearth of rental housing on Maui.

cvii Ray Miller, Friendly Isle Realty, Inc., (808) 553-3666, e-mail: raym@aoloha.net, http://www.molokairealty.com

cviii Ruth Chang & Associates, Inc., Honolulu (808) 735-9945, FAX 739-0696

cixPacific Business News, August 1999

cx LaCroix, Sumner J. *The Price of Paradise*, page 135 (Mutual Publishing, Honolulu, 1992)

cxi Kodani, Roy M., *Open House, a guide to buying and selling Hawaii real estate*, University of Hawaii Press, 1991, pg. 37

cxii Each island will have its own general plan and regional plans. On Oahu, the Department of Planning and Permitting will have copies of plans for public review. Request copies from each island planning department.

cxiii In purchasing a condominium, buyers should be aware of ongoing expenses associated with condominium ownership. In addition to mortgage payments, property taxes, insurance and utilities, most condo owners pay a monthly maintenance fee which covers landscaping, common area maintenance and a "contingency account" for major repairs to roof, common drives and pool or spa. These fees can run from $200 to $600 per month.

cxiv Ochwat, Tom, *Hawaii Real Estate Investment Guide*, page 17 (Hawaiian International Trade Publications)

cxv Counties are working to make permitting into a one-stop shop experience to speed up the process.

cxvi Martin Oliver, on Hawaii Island, is a buyer's agent, who tells us there are affordable properties available here. You may contact him at (808)962-9722; 936-1566 cell phone.

cxvii For more information on housing, upscale and low cost, designed for tropical and sub-tropical island living, contact Carey Smoot, owner-manager at (808)254-4002 in Honolulu.

cxviii For homestead defined see Black's Law Dictionary, Fourth Edition revised, 1968, West Publishing Co., pp. 866-867. The Hawaiian Homestead Act of 1924 provided for parcels of land to be made available to those of at least 50% Native Hawaiian blood on a leasehold only basis. Parcels are available for lease at $1.00 per year but the leaseholder is not able to secure clear title nor can such land be passed on in an inheritance (There is a mechanism for passing on the lease to a designated recipient.)

cxix Puna Water Services, Keaau Shopping Center, 982-8282

cxx Those persons who seeking privacy, even solitude, move as far down the road as the road goes, and not infrequently, a footpath further than road itself.

cxxi Informational literature from Ponds at Punalu'u.

cxxii Halas, Susan, "Senior Housing Complexes Planned on Maui," *Pacific Business News*, November 22, 1999

cxxiii For an examination of the impact of this process on the landscape of Honolulu, see Krauss, Bob, *High-Rise Hawaii*, Coward-McCann, Inc., New York 1969

cxxiv Oda, Francis, *The Price of Paradise*, Land Planning—What Might Hawaii Look and Feel like Years From Now? Pgs. 145-149

cxxv *Ibid.*

cxxvi Farrel, Bryan H., *Hawaii: The Legend That Sells*, University of Hawaii Press 1982

cxxvii See also Strategic Plan – Hilo-Hamakua Coast 2000

cxxviii Goodell, Bonnie, *Puna Community Development Plan*, 1995. For another look at future "rural town districts," see also Appendix B, Aloha Villages in *Hawaii Summit: Project 2011, Final Report*, Executive Office on Aging, State of Hawaii, 1998, p. 40

cxxix E.g., Kona Village, located in the northern area of the Platinum Coast, offers thatched roof houses with no TV and no phone, providing splendid isolation in the midst of a compound of such units, for a <u>mere</u> $300 per night. Ideal for honeymooners perhaps but not quite right for adventurous retirees on a budget. Other examples are the Hilton Hawaiian Village on Oahu and Waikoloa Village on the Big Island, neither one a village so much as a Disneyland for adults who fantasize village life for a weekend or two. See also Farrell, Bryan H., *Hawaii: The Legend That Sells*, University of Hawaii Press 1982

cxxx Despite extensive effort to secure such data, we found a noticeable lack of reliable data on in-migration and transplant residents.

cxxxi Cooper & Daws, *Land & Power*, University of Hawaii Press, 1990, Chapter 2. Also Callies, David L., *Land & Power*, University of Hawaii Press, 1990, "Dealing with Scarcity Land Use and Planning" pp. 131-145.

cxxxii Nil, Esme Infante, *The Honolulu Advertiser*, "Our families, our health", January 1, 2000

cxxxiii Danninger, Lyn, *Pacific Business News*, August 20, 1999

cxxxiv *The State of Hawaii Data Book 1998*

cxxxv *Ibid.*

cxxxvi Nutrition sites provide low cost meals for residents over 60 years of age. These nutrition sites are usually located in a senior center, community center or other meeting place. They are usually administered by the counties.

cxxxvii Fujita, Beverly, "The Big Island: A Healing Destination," *Spirit of Aloha*, March 2000

cxxxviii Monson, Valerie, "Accreditation Panel Lauds Maui Memorial," *The Maui News*, May 3, 1999

cxxxix Wilson, Christie, "Maui short on senior care," *The Honolulu Advertiser*, November 19, 2000. The article reported on a Senior Choices 2000 conference attended by 300 people at the Kaunoa Senior Center.

cxl "Hawaii health plans take national honors," *Newsweek*, November, 1999—naming Kaiser Permanente Hawaii and Health Plan Hawaii, a HMO of the Hawaii Medical Service Association

(HMSA), in the top 40 HMOs by the National Committee for Quality Assurance (NCQA).

cxli Executive Office on Aging, Honolulu

cxlii Executive Office on Aging, Senior Newsletter, 1999

cxliii Ibid.

cxliv Pukui, Mary Kawena and Samuel H. Elbert, *New Pocket Hawaiian Dictionary*, University of Hawaii Press, Honolulu 1997

cxlv Hawaii County Executive Office on Aging, Silver Bulletin, 1999

cxlvi Movie Buffs will argue endlessly among themselves that the scene in question was filmed at a small inaccessible beach near the "Blowhole."

cxlvii The Honolulu computer system for tee time signups was recently victim of hackers trying to get more golf time. See Blackman, Karen, *The Honolulu Advertiser*, "System hackers tee off Ala Wai golfers," October 28, 2000.

cxlviii Masuoka, Brandon, *The Honolulu Advertiser*, "Two arrested in tee-time racket; Ala Wai golfers may face arrest," June 20, 2000.

cxlix Plasch, Bruce S., "Should We Allow So Many Golf Course to be Built? in *The Price of Paradise*, Mutual Publishing, 1992, pp. 163-167.

cl Kayal, Michele, *The Honolulu Advertiser*, "State ending Ala Wai golf," October 1, 2000.

cli Slack Key is a style of tuning and playing the guitar adopted by Hawaiian cowboys (*paniolos*).

clii Loosely defined as a combination of Jamaican and Hawaiian.

cliii Yoshida, George, *Hawaii's BEST Cookbook on Fried Rice*, Big Island Printers, Hilo, HI.

cliv Corum, Ann Kondo, *Ethnic Foods of Hawaii*, The Bess Press, Honolulu 2000

clv Clarke, Joan, *Local Food, What to Eat in Hawaii*, Namkoong Publishing, Honolulu 1997, pg. 18

clvi *Ibid.* page 23

clvii *Ibid.* page 33

clviii Horowitz, Lenore W., *Hawaii Kauai Underground Guide*, Papaloa Press 1998. See also Farmer's Markets, pg. 82

clix Katsu is a Japanese bar-b-que sauce

clx We have no idea why this diet, a basic "eat-more-foods-with-fewer-calories" diet, is called the <u>Hawaii</u> diet. It is a popular diet this year. The book and infomercial are seen and sold in many locations in Hawaii.

clxi Zagat Survey,Hawaii Restaurants 1998

clxii They are members of the Hawaii Restaurant Association.

clxiii"When you wish upon a Star," Music by Leigh Harline, lyrics by Ned Washington. Original copyright 1940 by Bourne Co. From Disney's "Pinocchio."

clxiv *The Robb Report*, Olympic Publishing Co.

clxv Joe Correa Realty, Inc, 10 Lono Street, Hilo (808)961-6567, FAX 959-5487

clxviOn one occasion Toffler applied his general thesis to the case of Hawaii taking pains to articulate his thesis and fashioned a possible solution in the form of "Anticipatory Democracy" Toffler, Alvin, "Anticipatory Democracy and the Prevention of Future Shock," pp. 74-78 in Geo. Chaplin and Glenn Paige eds, *Hawaii 2000*, University of Hawaii Press, 1974. See also Toffler, Alvin, *Future Shock*, Random House, Inc., June 1970.

clxvii Dychtwald, Ken, Ph.D., *Age Power; How the 21st Century will be Ruled by the New Old*, Jeremy P. Tarcher/Putnam, New York 1999, p.1

clxviii Ibid, p. 19

clxix In a 1999 seminar/panel on health care for the elderly we posed the following question: "How many believe Hawaii is prepared for the impact of baby boomers on the local health care systems? Not a single hand out of some 50 persons went up as those who should know spoke volumes with their silence.

clxx *Hawaii Summit: Project 2011, Final Report* 1998, Executive Office on Aging, State of Hawaii, p. 4

clxxi Dychtwald, Ken, Ph.D., *Age Power; How the 21st Century will be Ruled by the New Old*, Jeremy P. Tarcher/Putnam, New York 1999, p. 29

clxxii Morgan, Joseph, *Hawaii: A Unique Geography*, The Bess Press, 1996, pp. 81-82 and 85-87

clxxiii Ibid, p. 226, See also Native Hawaiian Sovereignty Movement

clxxiv This recent (May 2000) Supreme Court decision mandated the right of Hawaii residents and non-Native Hawaiians to vote in matters pertaining to the Trustees of the Office of Hawaiian Affairs. It meant that in Hawaii qualified voters with no Native blood nor ancestral history could participate in the election of OHA trustees (See *The Honolulu Advertiser* statewide election coverage 11/6/00 through 11/8/00. Spokespersons on both sides dispute the scope and implications of the decision. Clearly, however, it reaches the thorny political issue of who is a Native Hawaiian and who should govern their fate. Incoming prospective residents will likely have a say in this matter and those nouveau arrives could determine the outcome of future elections. See Rice vs Cayetano, and commentary releases from Trask and OHA, TV talk shows, op.ed. etc.

clxxv Chaplin, George and Glenn D. Paige, *Hawaii 2000*, University of Hawaii Press, 1973, Smyser, A.A., *Hawaii's Future in the Pacific, Disaster, Backwater or Future State?*, The East-West Center, 1988, Krauss, Bob, *High-Rise Hawaii*, Coward-McCann, Inc., New York 1969

clxxvi *Hawaii Summit: 2011 Project, Final Report 1998*, State of Hawaii Office of Aging, p. 3, 5

clxxvii Dickinson, Peter A., *Retirement Edens*, American Association for Retired Persons, 1987 clxxviii Duchemin, John, The Honolulu Advertiser, "Japanese investors trickle back to Islands, 11/5/2000

clxxix Rice vs Cayetano See also SB 2899 also known as the Akaka Bill. The Reconciliation bill introduced by Senator Akaka and supported by Senator Inouye and Representatives Neil Abercrombie and Patsy Mink was adopted by the Congress in 2000. Public hearings were held throughout the islands with cheers, jeers, protests and accolades from various factions of the Native Hawaiian population. Results ran the gamut from one extreme to the other.

clxxx The legislation (SB 2899 and H.R. 4904) were co-terminously introduced in the U.S. Senate by Senators Daniel Akaka (D-Hawaii) and Daniel Inouye (D – Hawaii) through the Indian Affairs Committee and by Representative Neil Abercrombie (D – Hawaii) through the Committee on Resources on July 20, 2000. The bill as amended was passed in 2000.

clxxxi Morgan, Joseph, *Hawaii: A Unique Geography*, The Bess Press, Honolulu 1996 p. 227, 228

clxxxii See Chapter Two FN 15 re. Haunani Kay Trask and her brand of provincialism, secessionist logic, and Native Hawaiian independence. "Hawaii, which has a long history of welcoming new immigrants and diversity, has begun to show signs of strain," *Hawaii Summit: Project 2011*, 1998, p. 5

clxxxiii Dychtwald, PhD, Kenneth, *Age Power*, Tarcher/Putnam 1999

clxxxiv AARP Policy Manual, Chapter One

clxxxv In the *Price of Paradise*, Robert Gardner writes that "...of people living in Hawaii who had lived elsewhere one year earlier, usually about eighty percent had been in another state, only twenty percent in a different country...It thus appears that our migrants (the people here now who weren't here before) are predominantly from the Mainland."